Sandra Fazio is also the author of:

"The Diaries of a Conscious Parent:
One mother's journey to raising herself through
her daughter's essence"

Download a free eBook copy at: sandrafazio.com/subscribe

Permission to Feel

Inspirational Poems for
Your Awakened Consciousness

SANDRA FAZIO

Foreword by Dr. Shefali Tsabary
NYT Bestselling Author of The Conscious Parent
and The Awakened Family

BALBOA.
PRESS
A DIVISION OF HAY HOUSE

Balboa Press books may be ordered through booksellers or by contacting:

Balboa Press
A Division of Hay House
1663 Liberty Drive
Bloomington, IN 47403
www.balboapress.com
1 (877) 407-4847

Print information available on the last page.

ISBN: 978-1-9822-2870-5 (sc)
ISBN: 978-1-9822-2872-9 (hc)
ISBN: 978-1-9822-2871-2 (e)

Library of Congress Control Number: 2019906868

Balboa Press rev. date: 10/23/2019

Dedication

To my daughter

You are my reason and purpose for all I am

Through your birth, I have awakened
Through your love, I have received
Through your spirit, I have transformed

You are my spiritual guide and earth angel

Thank you for choosing me to walk this
path alongside you

Thank you for loving me through
all my imperfections in this human form

I am forever blessed and humbled
you chose me to be your mom

Advance Acclaim for

Permission to Feel

"The poems Sandra Fazio has gifted us with in this present volume are evocative of our essential selves, calling to us in language that addresses our souls. Through her poems, she reminds us that no matter how entrenched or unaware we may be in the helter-skelter pace of our technological era, our lives are nevertheless at every instant bathed in mystery. Her poetry is intended to awaken us to the ongoing presence of this mystery".

- **Dr. Shefali Tsabary,** *Clinical Psychologist and New York Times best-selling author of The Conscious Parent and The Awakened Family,* **United States**

"Sandra Fazio offers a unique vantage point with her new book. Through poetry she gives the reader an opportunity to peer more closely into their own soul rhythms. The titles of the poems alone invite contemplation. I see this book being utilized in tandem with self-reflection for those interested in perceiving their own unfolding life in a deeper and wider way. It is a truly beautiful contribution to our world".

- **Annie Burnside,** *Author of Soul to Soul Parenting and From Role to Soul,* **United States**

"Through this book of poetry, Sandra Fazio opens up her heart and soul and allows us to know the depths of her wisdom. This collection of discrete poems create a magnificent mosaic of honesty, empathy and compassion. She simultaneously shines a warm light on the dark places within each of us and illuminates a path forward toward authentic knowing, accepting, appreciating and loving of both self and others.

I highly recommend this book for anyone who is parenting, has been parented or is looking for a deeper sense of connection to life from within".

- **Carrie Contey**, *PhD and author of CALMS: A guide to soothing your baby*, **United States**

"Sandra's words have a way of luring you into her poetry and making you feel a part of it—dancing in the music of it—until your soul cracks open to transformation and gives you *Permission to Feel*. By sharing her own experiences in this uplifting compilation, Sandra organically leads you to recognize and unravel hidden knots in your physical, emotional, and mental memory. Her heartfelt dedication is truly enjoyable, magical, and transformational"!

- **Roma Khetarpal**, *educator, founder of Tools of Growth, and author of the award-winning book The "Perfect" Parent*, **United States**

"This collection of life and self, poured out onto pages with words woven together so brilliantly, is a gift – a beautiful and transformative gift. The experience of being shown that you've been sleeping, the jarring reality of a wake-up call, and the passage out of illusion and into truth can feel so solitary. But this collection through *Permission to Feel* makes you feel seen, heard, collected. Sandra's words highlight the truth - which is most personal - is also indeed most universal that 'I see you and I get you, because I am you.' Truth".

- **Dr. Vanessa Lapointe**, *registered psychologist, parenting expert, and mom*, **United States**

"In writing such deeply personal and inquisitive poetry, Sandra has invited us to point our own spiritual and investigative compasses inward. No matter the subject you are contemplating, she guides her readers on an introspective journey to discover what we feel, why we feel it, and in some cases, what we might do about it. Working through a book like this is for the brave; these are not passive poems! They are calls-to-action for your innermost self. They will wash over you in waves as you glean the layers of understanding and enjoyment, simultaneously feeling the stirrings of that activist heart awakening. Can you heed that yearning? Are you ready to listen? I think you already did heed the call! I think you are already listening! After all, you are already holding the book...enjoy".

- **Emily A. Filmore**, *Author of The Marvelous Transformation: Living Well with Autoimmune Disease, Co-author of Conversations with God for Parents and Parenting through Divinity,* **United States**

"Sandra has an uncanny ability to combine soulful poetic writing and parenting principles in a way that will both soothe and inspire you. You'll return to this treasure over-and-over again".

- **Suzi Lula**, *Best Selling Author, The Motherhood Evolution: How Thriving Mothers Raise Thriving Children,* **United States**

"As a relationship therapist, this is a must read for every mother. Sandra Fazio invites you on a journey through the muddiness and messiness yet untethered spiritual depth of motherhood. Her poetic words sizzle with courage and unadorned truth that reverberate with heart grabbing uncanniness—that she's traversed your emotional cracks, has gone through your same struggles.

Permission to Feel will open places in you that may have been long buried under the seemingly stultifying to-dos of parenting and awaken you in the most profound ways, to the sacred transformative qualities that can be uncovered and discovered in the mother-child relationship".

- **Amy-Noelle**, *Relationship Therapist, Founder of Power-Truth Living*, **United States**

"Sandra Fazio's book *Permission to Feel* is a collection of powerful poems that took my breath away. It's a must read for everyone, especially those on the ever-evolving journey of parenting.

Each and every page has Sandra's heart sprinkled all over it. The magnetic pull of the words clearly created with love, truth and wisdom is undeniable.

Sandra's magical poems are relatable, reaffirming, deeply resonate and have a permanent spot on my nightstand. *Permission to Feel* showcases Sandra's divine light and special writing talent brilliantly".

- **Vibha Arora**, *MFT, Life Coach*, **United States**

"Oh, how lovely the pen that Sandra holds! Her prose flows effortlessly and with each precise word choice, she takes the reader deep into her world, her wounds, and onto her healing path. With her, goes the reader into their own inner landscape if they allow their hearts to open. Sandra is dedicated to revealing herself through her vulnerable writing and it is a gift to readers who choose to explore this book! Gratitude to Sandra for putting this out in *The Universe* so we may all journey inward, all the while recognizing none of us are alone".

- **Annette Kane-Shine**, *Executive Coach/Parent Coach, Trainer, Speaker*, **United States**

"*Permission to Feel* is lyrically beautiful and timelessly moving, as it traces the journey that no one wants to take…one that challenges our narratives and ideologies, brings front and center our authentic experiences of fear, worry, truth and triumph, and ultimately awakens the soul. We don't always get to choose what happens in this life, but we can choose to grow in compassion and wisdom.

Sandra Fazio provides a striking example of this as she chronicles her own path to consciousness, alignment, parenting and a host of relatable life events. The book offers poignant and transformational poetry, prose and musings that cut directly to the heart. Her suggestions ring clear and true because she knows the territory intimately in all its pain and promise and has given us the gift of sharing it".

- *Joe Atalig*, *Transformational Speaker and Coach, Founder of Love Wave Live!,* **United States**

"Sandra Fazio is a master of words. Her poetry brings about deep reflections and is an expansion of music to one's heart and soul. *Permission to Feel* allows us to access the melodic and deep sacred connection to our essence".

- *Karol Miranda*, *Therapist and Body Talk Practitioner,* **Brazil**

"*Permission to Feel* is purely exquisite and is for anyone who has feared the range and / or the depths of their feelings - you can see where they may lead. Though we are all unique, we are woven of the same thread, in the fabric of creation. We are learning to live an authentic life. Each page within contains a place to rest, reflect and warmed within your spirit. All emotions are a messenger and they worked their way through Sandra and onto the page masterfully"!

- *Brigid Hopkins*, *Author of Feathers of a Phoenix and Clarity Coach,* **United States**

"Sandra's writing is breathtaking; a true gem. Her poems are real, raw, and take us on a journey of insight and reflection about living an awakened life. In *Permission to Feel*, Sandra translates with mastery the experiences we have as mothers, bringing to life the words and emotions that are inside us, waiting to be heard, embraced and healed. Her words open the doors to our own authentic core and personal evolution".

- **Patricia Barros**, *MD, Empowerment Coach for Mothers, Certified Parent Coach,* **United States**

"Sandra's writing is insightful, raw, and deeply heartfelt. I can't help but to reflect deeply on my own life experience as I read each of her poems".

- **Eric D. Greene**, *Parent Coach,* **United States**

"Powerful, raw and moving! *Permission to Feel* is a beautiful book of poetry that will become a compassionate and warm companion when you need uplift and reconnection to your authentic self and be reminded of: 'everything you are and all you ever need is already seeded within your soul'".

- **Anna Seewald**, *M. Ed, Host of the Authentic Parenting podcast,* **United States**

"Sandra's words are so real and relatable it feels as if I am being spoken to by a close friend who knows the exact right thing I need to hear at the exact right moment. Her insights wrap around me like a big hug showing me I'm not alone. Her words have the power to permeate through me, reaching every cell in my body, initiating the healing I have craved so deeply. Sandra is a true guide".

- **Kelly Garvey**, *Photographer,* **United States**

"Poetry is such a beautiful way to express our deep feelings and allow others to see our vulnerability. Sandra does both in this collection of inspiring and uplifting poems. I'd encourage clients and friends alike to read these poems when searching for the right words to explain their feelings or hoping to feel empowered while on their healing journey".

- *Mercedes Samudio, LCSW, Author of Shame-Proof Parenting: Find your unique voice, feel empowered, and raise whole, healthy children,* **United States**

"This book of Sandra's poetry is a portal to knowing, believing, and feeling - in every cell of your being - that you are not alone. No matter how difficult your parenting journey has been, reading Sandra's poetry, you will have your experiences reflected to you. It will bring you comfort in the moment of reading, and fuel you for the next steps of your journey ahead. You will find yourself and be compelled and able to give yourself just what you need from you. Even when and especially when you feel most isolated in your experiences as a parent, you will see and feel yourself accepted just as you are. This collection is your haven. I highly recommend you keep it in easy reach".

- *Sheryl Stoller, Parent Coach at Stoller Parent Coaching and The Center for Identity Potential to parents of (un)identified gifted and twice-exceptional children with intense behaviors and emotions,* **United States**

"Sandra's writing has a way of peeling back the layers of our hearts to peer inside to all the wonder and magic that appears. Sandra has such a tender approach in her writing because as we slowly uncover the painful parts hidden in our hearts, she has a way to add comfort and ease to the process to replace the pain with love. Her soul shines through in all of her work and allows us, as the reader, to shine as well. It's a magical and reciprocal process where we are safe to feel – allowing us to float through life as we gently release the sandbags that are weighing us down."

- **Kelly Hutcheson**, *Life Coach and Counselor,* **United States**

"This beautiful poetry manuscript is written with so much heart. *Permission to Feel* raises critical issues that many of us have experienced in the world of parenting, raising children and growing ourselves. Sandra touches on the many trials and tribulations helping her readers to tease out their own unspoken truth. This is raw, connecting, moving and helpful. I felt myself emotional, reflective and feeling deeply connected to the author and her message. There is something for everyone. The love that comes off the pages as one reads through these beautiful pieces is truly moving.

Anyone raising children today will find this book a treasure in many ways, helping you to be reflective, observant, introspective and moved".

- **Sue DeCaro**, *Heart-Centered Parent and Life Coach, Educator and Speaker, helping individuals, organizations, and families around the globe to navigate through life's daily challenges,* **United States**

"Sandra shares herself so courageously, so beautifully and so lovingly in her writings. She is able to articulate what so many of us feel, in parenting and in life. When we are struggling, we can feel so alone. But Sandra helps our hearts to know that we are not alone. Rather in her, we have a friend on this path of life, someone who is shining her light brightly for us to follow".

- **Erin Taylor**, *Parent, Life and Business Coach, Author and Speaker,* **United States**

"Sandra has a beautiful way of drawing you in with her eloquent words and deep insights. As you read her poems you can't help but feel more connected to your heart and soul. Her writing invites you on a journey to rediscover what it means to be a fully evolved human being. She reminds us that our lives are filled with contrasts - both highs and lows, joy and sorrow, love and loss. It is often when we shift our perspective that we can fully embrace the totality of the human experience".

- **Kristen Harcourt**, *Professional Coach and Speaker,* **Canada**

"Each word that comes through Sandra touches the soul of the one who is reading it. She is a gifted poet, a beautiful storyteller and a woman who shares from a place of love, vulnerability and passion. She creates with intention and it is felt in these pages.

I consider discovering Sandra and her words a true blessing in my life. A must read for anyone who loves to be taken on a journey through written word. Be prepared to have your soul moved".

- **Tania Joy Antonio**, *Author of The Affirmation Station and The Magical Mystical Warrior Of Love,* **Canada**

"These poems are so honest and raw. At times, I felt like Sandra was directly talking to me. She has the power to make it relatable no matter your age, gender or ethnicity. There is something for everyone in here"!

- **Florencia Rodriguez**, *Clinical Psychologist,* **Chile**

"I have followed Sandra's work for several years, now. I felt called to her messages, so true, so honest, so heartfelt. She has been a beacon of light to me, personally and professionally and should our 'real-life' distance not be the 5000+ miles that it is, I would want to be in her company as often as possible.

Sandra has been generous enough to share her poems previously, and I have benefited greatly through reading and re-reading her work. Her two poems 'Trusted my knowing', and 'Everything always works out' are like a large comfort blanket, full of truth!

She has this gift of knowledge; of knowing, of being so in touch with the human soul that her words sing from the page, leaping off the manuscript and straight into my heart. If you want to feel centered, inspired, delighted; if you want to grow, smile, understand more - then do not pass this poetry book by without adding it to your collection".

- **Dr. Fay Sallaba**, *General Practitioner and Parent Coach*, **England and Germany**

"This wholehearted inspirational book reveals how speaking your truth and releasing your feelings can act as a birth canal to every woman's most authentic spirit. In each one of these poems that Sandra writes, every being can find a source of wisdom, hope and a conduit to empower the most forbidden of human rights...the *Permission to Feel*".

- **Andrea González,** *Clinical Psychologist, Conscious Parent Coach, Former President of the Guatemalan Psychological Association,* **Guatemala**

"Sandra shares her journey with a heartfelt passion that invites us to read along and reflect on our truths as we awaken alongside her. Her words flow with beauty and ease and serve as a companion providing inspiration as we move along our conscious path".

- **Karen Vallejos, United States**

"Sandra Fazio is a compassionate and wise soul with a special gift to touch another's heart. *Permission to Feel* is an exquisite compilation of Sandra's work that allows her deep wisdom to beautifully flow into her poetry. If willing, these writings have the ability to touch deep places within the reader's heart and soul and awaken the divine within".

- **Amanda Votto**, *PA-C, Mindfulness Teacher, Speaker and Coach,* **United States**

"*Permission to Feel* is a must read for anyone traveling the challenging path of conscious awakening. I love Sandra's poetry. Her wise, intimate account of personal transformation assures us we are not alone and that who we are at any given moment is enough and exactly who we should be".

- **Debbie Maron**, *Certified Professional Life Coach,* **United States**

"It is rare and courageous when an author is willing to open up and disclose her vulnerabilities as freely as Sandra has done in this compelling collection of reflections on her parenting journey. She exposes the struggles and challenges of her journey toward authenticity, loving and accepting herself as whole, and invites us to do the same. Her expressions of clarity and hope are an inspiration to all parents who yearn to be and do their best".

- **Georgia P. DeClark**, *Certified Parent Coach, Preschool Teacher and Director,* **United States**

"Through Sandra's poetry, we witness her unrelenting devotion to authenticity and her unconditional acceptance of life's rich and varied experiences as the path to self-discovery and self-acceptance. Through *Permission to Feel*, we are encouraged to embark on our own journey of inner exploration, to fully embrace all of life's messiness, and to cultivate self-compassion, clarity, and personal growth, and therefore our own transformation.

By sharing her own vulnerability, Sandra reminds us that we are not alone. This book is sacred space being held for you. Allow yourself the gift of receiving it".

- ***Jenifer Chase, United States***

"Sandra's poetry is the very essence of an awakened heart poured out on the page! I reference her in moments of judgment, self-criticism and shame. An anchor to cling to when the seas of life and mothering get rough, this compassionate collection mirrors the depth of our shared longing for acceptance and worthiness - just as we are".

- ***Cory Thomsen***, *Certified Professional Co-Active Coach*, **United States**

"Sandra has a magical way with words, each poem touching my heart with grace and vulnerability. As a mother of a child with extra needs, each word resonated, each poem breaking me open and healing my heart. I am grateful to Sandra and her raw, honest storytelling".

- ***Kylie Johnston***, *Certified Parent Coach, Heart Centered Parenting and Teaching*, **New Zealand**

"Permission to Feel is like a warm hug and a light shining on a dark path at the same time. Sandra beautifully captures the day to day emotions of parenting and sheds conscious light on it to see the blessings amongst the tough moments. *Permission to Feel* is not just for parents but for anyone wanting to live a more awakened, mindful and grounded life. I'm so grateful to have these to read for inspiration and support. Thank you, Sandra".

- *Jacquie Dunbar, Mindfulness and Meditation Teacher,* **Australia**

"Sandra Fazio's, *Permission to Feel,* is a collection of beautiful poems that are filled with love, compassion and inspiration in many areas of our journey in life. Her work authentically shares her experiences to encourage others on their own journey of consciousness. Sandra's words gently challenge the reader to allow themselves to feel and move through those hard feelings that we oftentimes try to avoid. Truly an inspiration that connects to your soul"!

- *N. Jones, United States*

"In *Permission to Feel,* Sandra Fazio inspires us with her profound insights and observations of personal growth. Sandra's deeply expressive poetry resonates ubiquitously with the unspoken thoughts of those traversing parenthood and life as a whole. I highly recommend this book to anyone seeking a shift in perspective away from conditioned beliefs whilst aspiring to become a higher version of self".

- *Selina E. Rovinsky, Conscious Parent and Educator,* **United States**

"Sandra's dedication to self-evolution and growth is remarkable. Her ability to take a deep dive within, to look at the bigger lesson and growth opportunity in every situation makes her an amazing mother and perfect proponent of conscious parenting. This book of poems is a wonderful accounting of a mother's struggle to grow herself through parenting. Bravo"!

- *Melissa Volz, LPC,* **United States**

"Sandra's book in my hands has been a divine self-care appointment. Each day I'd look forward to reading a chapter of Sandra's poems. One night I stayed up late just to read the whole book over again. So many of the poems resonate with me. Reading them feels therapeutic.

I've been working on self-healing for years now. I've made so much progress and yet a couple triggers keep me going around in circles. *Permission to Feel* helped me identify why I keep repeating the patterns. I am deeply grateful to have felt my heart and head harmonize and to have felt safely held in the process.

Permission to Feel is rich with empathy, enlightenment and comfort. I'll be reading the poems over again, and again, in times of reflection".

- **Lelia Schott**, *Synergy Parenting Resources, Certified Parent Coach,* **South Africa**

"Sandra's strength and perseverance shines through in stunning clarity in her writing. Her open heart touches the reader through images we find familiar and reflective of our own challenges. I'm inspired by the vulnerable sharing that comes forth in her poetry and know that Sandra is a leader in our global village of awakened motherhood. *Permission to Feel* is a book of wisdom teachings in practice and helps the reader integrate new concepts into their busy journey through parenthood and beyond".

- **Beth Rowles**, *Founder of The Family Alchemists,* **United States**

"*Permission to Feel* is a rich multitude of deeply personal insights that is sure to inspire and fuel your own self-exploration. Sandra's wisdom is a gift to your higher self and invites you to be more you"!

- **Rick Morrison**, *Author of The Hug Store and Founder of Hug The Moment, an educational 501c3,* **United States**

"This book is a treasure of inspiration! Sandra Fazio is a mama in the trenches who has put into words what many parents of struggling kiddos sometimes think, feel, and experience. *Permission to Feel* is a collection of writings encouraging us to keep searching, hoping, and praying for our miracle of healing".

- **Shawna Pulver,** *FDN-P,* **United States**

Foreword

Dr. Shefali Tsabary

I feel quite certain that there has never been a time in the history of literature when the sharing of poetry was more needed than it is in our world today. We live in an era where we are increasingly consuming data without the time or space to process how all of this relates to our souls.

In our quest for progress, we have forgotten the most important aspect of our existence—our relationship to our essence. It's here that poetry, with its ability to synthesize information through metaphor, allows us to develop a synergy between the logical and creative aspects of our being. In doing so, it creates a portal to look within and unveil aspects of our essence that would otherwise remain buried in the chaos and din of our everyday existence.

The poems Sandra Fazio has gifted us with in this present volume are evocative of our essential selves, calling to us in language that addresses our souls. Through her poems, she reminds us that no matter how entrenched or unaware we may be in the helter-skelter pace of our technological era, our lives are nevertheless at every instant bathed in mystery. Her poetry is intended to awaken us to the ongoing presence of this mystery.

Sandra's particular collection of poems is grounded in an aspect of our lives that has been, and continues to be, of special relevance in my own journey - the ever-mysterious connection between parent and child. This connection was brought to light in a particularly moving manner in a poem about parenting offered to the world by the Lebanese-American writer, poet, and artist Kahlil Gibran. The insights he shared concerning parenting in his little book *The Prophet* touched the lives of millions. But I have to wonder how many of those who saw something beautiful in his words realized the extent to which the approach to parenting he advocated constitutes a radical upturning of the way almost every family in culture after culture, country after country, goes about the responsibility of bringing up their children.

My own insights into what it takes to parent consciously, which is the opposite of the emotionally reactive and dictatorial way in which so many of us address our children, dovetails with the approach to children taken in *The Prophet*. It's for this reason that I'm thrilled to see how Sandra has built on these revolutionary insights, developing and filling out what Gibran teaches us in ways both practical and inspiring.

In my first book *The Conscious Parent,* and my two succeeding books, I showed that it isn't so much we who are meant to teach our children, but our children who have come here to be *our* teachers. They enter our lives not so that we can produce carbon copies of ourselves who will fulfill those hopes and dreams we have been unable to fulfill, thus completing us, but so that we can see reflected in the way we relate to them all the ways in which we failed to grow up when we were children, the objective being to complete the journey of maturing into authentic adults through our interactions as a family from day to day.

Sandra writes of how this moment we are in right now is an opportunity to see who we truly are in our deepest being, so that we might align with this in our everyday activities.

Shefali

Dr. Shefali Tsabary,
Clinical Psychologist and
New York Times best-selling author of
The Conscious Parent and The Awakened Family

Preface

With the plethora of books out in the world, I am truly humbled that mine landed on your heart at this very moment. As precious as time is, I am equally honored that you have created the space and energy to allow my work to share a spot in your (inner) world.

Over the past few decades, I have been on a path to discover and evolve into my highest self, while expressing my truth through every experience of my life. I may not have always realized it, yet when I reflect back, I can now see more clearly the breadcrumbs and patterns of my own evolution. What has more recently catapulted me even deeper into the dive of awakening to my true self, and that has broken me down while breaking me open, has been particularly my journey of motherhood.

Prior to motherhood, I was out exploring and enjoying the world with a zest for all things self-growth. I had really no limitations, no constraint and no anchors in my life, and I was able to venture, travel and endeavor my path and purpose here on Earth - all the while not knowing it would be motherhood where my soul's purpose would be found. Becoming a mother at the age of 39, I chose to quit my then advertising and sales career to be home full-time with my daughter. I had such a fantasy of what motherhood was going to look like - thinking I had laid out all the stones to receive it in the exact way I had envisioned – only to come and find that it would be the very thing that would have to break me down to actually wake me up. And, despite this awakening, I still find myself in the muck and magic in any given day.

My daughter sees a lot of my daily imperfections. She sees my despaired moments at times, amongst my conscious ones, because to be the most authentic example of a human being is to show her that life is not always going to be easy, but it is how we ease into life that we can juice out the lessons. As long as I remain most awake in those trying moments, I also know I need to keep attuning to self-love and self-acceptance – during the ebbs and flows, the falling and hitting the ground – reminding myself that I'm not at all here to be "perfect". Rather I'm here to learn and grow and experience the depths of what I'm meant to—so that I can rise to into my highest self.

I know that *The Universe* gave me a girl because I was meant to see myself so much more deeply from the eyes of this divine and wise soul – who I personally feel, know and believe has walked this journey with me in many past lives. To some, this may seem a little abstract and airy-fairy, but I don't hold an ounce of doubt and trust we both called each other into this life form to continue what we had started long ago. Every day, I try to practice the practice of self-acceptance and self-love as a mom and a human being. I fall and rise. I veer off course and course correct. I have guilt and grace. My daughter is here to remind me every day how much I have yet to still grow because this isn't an end-all, be-all destination. This is not a one-time experience. It's a continuum of self-discovery, and I'm sure I'm going to have many more lifetimes at this experience—just in different life forms.

I've become deeper in my truth and my self-love and self-acceptance through my journey into motherhood than any other place to-date. Much of this has been experienced through the cathartic healing of writing poetry, which is a kind of love language of my own soul that I never knew existed prior to being a mom. Poetry has become kind of a medium—a language that I feel *The Universe* speaks through me. It gives me reflection and resonance of my own experiences so I can actually observe it from a higher perspective, outside of the physical self.

Parenthood may have brought you the same experience. Perhaps a relationship, to which you have devoted your life, has ended or is on unsteady ground. You could have had a health scare or received news of a loved one who passed on, and as a result, you are feeling fearful or maybe even losing hope for the future. Maybe you are feeling financially insecure, or perhaps working in a job that is depleting you instead of fulfilling you.

Every pain will be and feel different to each of us. Yet there is one thing I can undoubtedly say - pain is one of the most powerfully transformative ingredients on the trajectory of self-growth.

However we are meant to awaken deeper to our true self through the portal of our pain, I wholeheartedly believe there is always a silver lining and purpose in all experiences we encounter, just as there is a lesson to be learned through the unknown of each moment. We ultimately get to choose the lens which we view our experiences. We get to choose our vantage point and can adjust the scope of our lens, viewing our situation through lack or abundance, trial and triumph, opposition and opportunity, burden and blessing, failure and fortune. The way we choose to view our experiences equips us to harness our inner power without relinquishing it to a person or situation, unless we of course consciously choose to do so.

We do this concurrently with recognizing that there is an unwavering neutrality in the space between each perspective. Sometimes we will be in both places at the same time, and it is a very natural part of evolution. It's where our humanness and spiritual being emerge, and often where the magic of transformation occurs. How far one way or the other we swing the pendulum, then decide to stay in that space, is up to us. Because life is constantly changing, we know we will ultimately find our center.

While you will find an array of my poems reflecting the breakdown and breakthroughs of my motherhood journey, they also encompass interactions with my coaching clients, daily encounters in the world, random insights and curiosity, personal interpretations of wisdom teachings, keepsake memories of my journey, and an overall balancing of life as a whole between my humanness and my spirit. You will journey with me through my experiences of parent and child, pain and purpose, surrender and acceptance. From awakening and transformation to love and fear, my writing flows through all channels of life.

See, I never really "thought" of myself as a writer because for me writing isn't something I can "think" to do. It is something I feel and experience. What actually started off as blogging several years ago has since turned into poetry and inspirational memes, which you will find scattered throughout my book. I have found the form of my writing evolving simultaneously as I evolve. I didn't take any formal classes and it was never a lifelong dream of mine. It just happened and emerged organically through me following the birth of my daughter, as I realized quickly the mental fantasy in which I was living and how my motherhood journey "should" look and how it "should" go. Quite fooled was I, yet thankful. *The Universe*, in all its beautiful wisdom, had to get my attention to truly wake me up from my delusion.

Most of my poetry was written directly on my mobile phone as I lay on my couch when we lived in our Colorado apartment from 2016-2018, while my husband was traveling for extended periods with his work and my daughter was sleeping. Those moments of silence and that twenty-month transitional period for our family is where I did a lot of inner excavation. So much was going on personally in our lives and with our daughter's biomedical ("more needs") journey that I found myself retreating many times from the world outside to explore more deeply the world within me. It was in this sacred space that I would allow myself to just be, feel, experience, and melt into the truths that were brewing inside of me—the fears, the unknown, the pain, the anger, the frustrations, the desires, and the endless questions posed by my life. Writing poetry became a vessel of my soul's language to my own healing.

While many of my poems reflect my despair during that period of time, I now see more clearly through each passing day just how far I (and we as a family) have come during those unpredictable storms - consequently holding even deeper gratitude for this part of my journey. I realize I had to go through that phase to connect even closer to the truth of who I am – detaching more and more from my ego and tapping more deeply into my essence. The last poem in this book speaks to "How Far We Have Come" and as I wrote this poem, I could feel the weight roll off my shoulders and a deep sigh exude from my chest.

Presently, while we are no longer in such a deep transitional space, we are experiencing the fruits of our labor and most importantly seeing our daughter prosper and thrive so freely. A lot has been invested emotionally, energetically, physically, financially and spiritually to feel less anxious and more free, to be less resistant and more accepting and to show up less knowing and more trusting to the ever-unfolding process of life itself. This doesn't imply that there are not growing pains – of course there are and will continue so long as we are in this life form – yet I am merely becoming more of an observer who is witnessing our respective evolution and growth with awe-inspiring eyes and greater clarity. For I am not the same person I was when I started writing this book, nor will I be upon its publishing. Because each moment in between that space of time, I am continuing to uncover and discover deeper parts of my heart and soul.

I've often been asked whether I have any fear in sharing so openly as I do. To tell you "no" would be untrue. Yes, it has crossed my mind what others will think and how they will interpret my perspectives. My ego has often tried to seduce me into believing I will experience judgment and rejection as I share myself and my vulnerable experiences with the world. And I do realize the level of transparency I am exposing myself to when putting my writings out to the masses. Yet, after all washes aside and the essence arises, I know the deep sense of liberation that comes through self-expression. I am willing to take the risk, serve my purpose, and be a vessel and a voice of vulnerability. I don't feel that anything that comes through us is ours to own but rather ours to share. As we each share the seeds of our own journey with one another, consider the lush fields of connection we can sow for humanity.

A close companion and sanctuary, my writing is a space in which I meditate, witness, connect, and access my heart. It is where my metamorphosis happens and where I become more accepting of all of life's ebbs and flows. It is where I give myself *permission to feel*, pause and reflect, to experience greater inner clarity, to allow my humanness to emerge with my spirit, and to express any suppressed energy that isn't properly serving me. After writing, I begin to slowly nourish my emotional inner drought, revitalize my drained energy, and restore my sense of hope, faith, peace, trust, and acceptance that all is well and all is happening *for* me not *to* me.

Pouring my words onto the page gives me a reflection of my own experience and becomes my own mirror in which to witness my journey and growth. It is where I honor and love my being in all she is.

Â

This book is arranged so that you can find the precise poem you require in the moment you need it. There is no order to how you experience its flavors. I trust the way in which each poem is met by you will resonate exactly with where you are on your respective path.

My encouragement to you as you ingest the storytelling of my poetry is to discover your own unique vessel to connect to your truth, bring life to it, and be your own guiding light. May my words be not only a reflection and resonance of the fibers within you wherever you are on your journey, but become a sacred ground to mutually grow, evolve, transform, and accept the path of your journey as it was designed to be.

I trust whatever the reason you were drawn to my book that it fills your soul as it has my own. Whether you love poetry, you seek conscious inspiration, you are a parent, you follow me on social media, you know someone who told you about it, or you are looking to be heard and understood, your path brought you here in this moment with the common thread which is woven through the canvas of each page of our collective humanness.

It is all about being accepted for who we are, received in all our imperfections, experiencing permission to be in our truth, and feeling safe and not judged during our moments of unconsciousness. Basically, we just need to be told that all is well, and that we are not alone on this journey we call life.

I see you and I get you, because I am you. What matters most is that you are here investing the willingness to expand and grow, that you have shown up amid the battles and blessings, and we are sharing in this sacred space together.

With love,

Sandra

Permissions

Silence and Reflection

Trials and Transformation

Forgiveness and Love

Forgive what was.
Love what is.
Embrace what will be.

Dearest Inner Child

Are you a form of one's childhood
Where needs went unmet
Living through disconnection
To avoid and forget

A container of one's emotions
Where it was "wrong" to express
Living through denial
To resist and suppress

A reflection of past conditioning
Where projections took place
Living through fear
To protect its space

Where walls have been created
Like a shell with thick skin
Living through uncertainty
To trust letting anyone in

What if you are a version
Of my true self
Who has long carried the weight
Of everyone else

And after years of living inauthentically
You decide to break down the walls
To rediscover all along you are my soul
That has been yearning to live free

See it has been precisely through the path of my spiritual unfolding that I continue to learn how to lean more into the discomfort of my fears and feelings which then allows me to get more intimate with you, inner child, – *my soul*.

I can now see that you have always been the very core of my being – perhaps just disguised behind the conditions of the environment at any point in time in my life. Wearing different masks to protect me and guard my heart from the external influences.

So many times, over the course of my journey, I had been so hard on myself believing I should *"know better"* or that I was not *"ready, good or smart enough"*. And when I have gone down this path of thinking, I would lose you in the distance of the noise in my head, but there would still be an unspeakable feeling of you within my being saying *"it's okay" and "you are human,"* and *"you are enough, worthy and whole"*.

Thank you for carrying me this far, dearest inner child. Your courage and patience have been unwavering as you've allowed me almost five decades to ride the low and high tides of this life in the way I had to – to come home full circle to you again.

Permission granted.

Dearest Parents

I see you
I hear you
I feel you
I know you
I am you

We have been called into the lives of these incredible
souls because we are the only ones who could truly
traverse this difficult but rewarding path

Our children knew this when they called us
into their lives

They also knew we had a lot of lessons to learn and
they would be the only ones to teach us

⁓

I see you doing and being every moment of the day just to keep your head
above water

I see you walking on eggshells because you don't know what you may say
(or not say) that may trigger your child into a tantrum

I see you holding the space for your child during their big storms because
they feel "out of control"

I see you crying in your closet because you've had enough and feel helpless
with everything you are being that doesn't seem to work

I see you justifying and defending your child from your family, friends,
peers, strangers because they think you are not parenting "right"

I see you wishing you can run away for a day or longer and escape all that is being needed of you

I see you praying for silence because the external noise and needs of your child is competing with your internal voice - neither of them stopping

I see you getting frustrated and angry because it seems too much for any one person to carry the weight and responsibility

I see you questioning the how, the why, the when, the what - waiting for the next solution to bring ease your way

I see you worrying about the "labels" projected onto your child because it is misaligned to their true essence

I see you fearing the unknown and trusting the process that you've been called to on this journey of parenting a child's "more needs"

I see you feeling alone when you are with your friends and their kids are behaving well but your child is losing it over the smallest thing

I see you hesitating to travel because there is "no out" on the plane when your child triggers and people are less than compassionate towards you

I see you doing and being what it takes to help your child thrive

I see you searching for peace within and a day of "normalcy"

I see you finding the best way to connect with your child without it being and feeling so hard when they push back

I see you being so patient when your kid is hitting, kicking, screaming, spitting, swearing because you know they can't help themselves in that moment

I see you harboring guilt when you yell or get frustrated with your child because you've reached your threshold and have no more energy to spare

I see you conflicting with your partner because you both are torn at times with how to parent alike

I see you changing your day's plans because the emotions were too high, and it just feels safer to stay home

I see you spending unavailable funds to ensure you are providing the best care for your child

I see you setting boundaries but feeling conflicted internally with having empathy for your child and not wanting to be hard on them

I see you holding so much compassion for your child but not enough for yourself

I see you being hopeful that things will get easier - but it seems so distant especially when the emotional storms hit

I see you feeling sad when your child's feelings get hurt because you are hurting too

I see you believing that no matter what, you know your purpose is to guide your child to their highest self and not let them be or feel limited or "less than" because of their challenges

I see you advocating for your child at school when they seem to struggle and "the system" is not being flexible

I see you forgetting about taking care of yourself because all your focus is on helping your child feel calm

I see you tapping into your intuition because you sense deeper root causes to your child's emotional struggles

I see you trying to keep all the information together, so you can process and make sense of all you are learning on your parenting path

I see you wanting to ask for help but feeling scared at the same time because you feel no one really understands your situation

I see you seeking space to breathe and find silence

I see you loving your child with all your heart and soul knowing they chose you and you chose them in this lifetime

I see you being, doing, evolving, serving, allowing, trusting, feeling, expressing, unfolding, desiring, thinking, believing, experiencing, discovering, and searching

I see you discovering the parts that have yet to be found and felt inside of you

I see you breathing more freely as you ride the waves of your journey and all you have been called here to be and serve

I see you trusting that all things happen for a reason and knowing "this too shall pass" and that you and your child are both warriors

I see you and your child as whole, worthy and enough

Dearest Children

We are human
We are fallible
We will say and do the "wrong" things
For within, we are still children ourselves
Growing alongside you

Yet it is how we move through our mistakes
That the teachings we hope to impart
Will impact your depthless and compassionate heart

And as we stumble and fall
And find our own way back up
May you only stay connected to your spirit
Which is infinitely one with love

May you never dim your voice
Because of our inability to hear
May you trust your divine knowing
Not holding back your truths
In the name of fear

It is we who must take more breaths and pauses
Throughout the chaos of our day
Embodying the practice of mindfulness
When we feel triggered by "you"
In the slightest way

Though you may feel the projection
Of our intensified energy
Taking on more than you ever should have to
Because of the lack of our capacity and maturity

It's not you that we are resisting
It's ourselves and conditioned false beliefs
Our expectations and agendas at best
That cause our own suffering and grief

No child should hold the burdens
Of another's unhealed pain
Each child should live freely within their being
Harboring no self-inflicted guilt, shame or blame

When we feel helpless
We become demanding and unkind
Please call us out on it
Set your own boundaries
Remind us where to draw the line

To teach us how you need to be heard
Understood and held
Speaking up and respecting
Most importantly yourself

You have every right to feel angry
And even push us away
When the energy you are feeling
Is triggering you or making you feel afraid

It's our own fear that's talking
Our scared inner conditioning that projects
But when we tap into the truth of our heart
Are we only then able to feel our own heart's unrest

You may not always feel our love
In those moments of our despair
Yet in times of our own weakness
You teach us through your unconditional love and care

While there is never an excuse
For the way we may act
It's ours to own
And ultimately ours to course-correct

By asking
Let's do over
And make better
Let's start again
For tomorrow has yet to come
It's this new moment that we can begin

You are all beautiful souls
Whose hearts are beyond measure
The vibrance of your essence
Is a timeless treasure

You are love
You are light
You are our divine angels
Guiding the world so bright

Dearest True Self

Whenever you struggle to understand the storms in your life, I
invite you to look upwards toward the sun for it is always there
still shining bright even when the gray clouds are covering it.

And, as you continue upon your spiritual journey, when you may feel
disconnected from your humanness and forget how to allow yourself
to experience and express your emotions, I give you permission…

To allow all that moves through you

To be unapologetic in your pain without
self-judgment

To nurture the parts of your unforgotten soul

To release the shackles of guilt and shame that
have suffocated your true voice

To accept and love yourself as you are

To grant yourself …. *Permission to Feel.*

Pain and Purpose

*Pain is often an inner compass that
navigates us to our purpose.*

No Man's Land

Walking the path of self-truth
So lonely the journey can feel
Shedding skin along the way
In order for your soul to heal

Though you may be conflicted
And conditioned by the old
You always have a choice
In how "your story" gets told

Such freedom and liberation come
As you detach from your story
Creating newfound spaces within
To tap into your infinite glory

Let your soul breathe
Befriend your fears
Surrender the need to carry the unwanted burden
That's been weighing you down for years

Take to the wind
Take to the breeze
Open your arms wide
Fall to your knees

Allow your inner child to be heard and seen
Embrace and nurture its unhealed wounds
Hold the space for its tender needs
Be ever gentle and compassionate too

Know you will lose much along the way
But you will gain so much more
While some people drop out of your life
The Universe will bring you many like-minded ones to your door

Declare to *The Universe*
I'm reclaiming my voice, my truth, my light
See how it intelligently connects to your vibrational energy
To help you course-correct your life

No man's land is actually paradise for the soul
Where there are no edges
Just spaces
To experience its exponential growth

Trauma Has No Boundaries

Our cells are the carriers of our trauma
They store those memories so tight
Each time we encounter its energy
Our trauma resurrects and wants to fight

It gets our blood pressure high
Causes our limbs to go numb
Sometimes we lose consciousness
Due to the trauma that has been done

Whether the body has been beaten
Or the mind has been abused
The depths in which our trauma lives
Leaves us feeling wounded and confused

Trauma has no boundaries
It comes in all kinds of forms
From witnessing a tragedy
To how one may have been born

Or maybe our childhood reflected
A lot of scarcity and fear
And along our path of life
We lost someone we held so dear

Maybe it was in grade school
Where we were bullied and alone
Or perhaps the sounds of a child screaming
Cuts through us to the bone

Trauma is not a conversation
Many choose to have
For the fear of being judged
And feeling "lesser than"

Yet trauma is within us all
And deserves to be seen
When we feel rumbled by its tremors
May we trust it is for our awakening

Don't shame or hide
Don't guilt or condemn
For the traumatic memories inside
Must simply be dealt with

Our cells are the carriers of our trauma
They store those memories so tight
Each time we encounter its energy
We transform the pain into light

This Too Shall Pass

When you're in the thick
Of your deepest pain
There is a tendency to think
It will always be this way
This too shall pass

As you pay your bills
You see less than more
The worries build up
You can't take it anymore
This too shall pass

Your child acts out
Your patience wears thin
Helpless feelings
Begin to set in
This too shall pass

A loved one has transitioned
Your loss is immeasurable
The grief you experience
Is incomprehensible
This too shall pass

The opportunity you desired
Did not turn out your way
You feel defeated
And it's ruined your day
This too shall pass

A friend you call loyal
Has let you down
You wonder why suddenly
Why now
This too shall pass

Your partner is seeking
A different path
What once drew you to them
Now creates doubt and lack
This too shall pass

Your job requires
An out-of-state move
Leaving all you know
And start anew
This too shall pass

You long for change
And take the deep dive
Realize it's not that easy
Listening to your truth inside
This too shall pass

Repository of Pain

They had her young
She ingested their pain when they conceived
Though she was given a name
She was never truly received

They blamed
They accused
They shunned
They abused

She was the repository of their pain
Though her existence was constantly shamed
She will no longer tolerate or allow her essence
To be invisible or in vain

If she did "wrong" in their eyes
She was given a beating
Tormented deeply inside fearing her own life
She wouldn't even think of screaming

She wasn't taught how to love or connect
Or how to create a boundary
She was powerless and helpless
She was told she was the reason for their own suffering

She hesitated to use her voice
For fear that she would die
Her feelings didn't matter
She was told to shut up when she cried

Disconnection to her body
Was her way to protect her soul
Inflicting self-punishment
Was familiar to her from witnessing her parent's role

These patterns reflect the roots
Of her childhood trauma
Where she allowed others to beat her down
To stay small, cope and avoid all possible drama

Yet she knows beneath the surface of the
physical, mental and emotional pain
Lies her deeper connection to her innate wisdom
That she will no longer allow herself to repeat
the pattern of this perpetual blame

Despite the pain she's carried
And how much she's held inside
She is a true warrior who is beyond resilient
Who will no longer avoid, run away or hide

She's making a vow to reconnect
To her beautiful divinity
To be seen, to matter and be heard
For the sake of her own sovereignty

She will speak up
She will say no
She will draw the line
No longer will she surrender to being controlled

She will nurture her inner child
And hold great self-compassion
She will no longer fear or remain invisible
She will be seen and serve from a place of passion

She is worthy
She is whole
She is enough
She is connected to a greater source energy

This is her time to release
To allow
To trust
To tap into her limitless possibilities

Life isn't about being painless.

Rather about being painfully present to all moments before us so we can grow into our highest selves with deep clarity and purpose while we embrace this physical life form.

Sometimes It Feels Too Heavy

Sometimes it feels too heavy
The weight we are carrying around
Whether it's physical or emotional
The force of our burdens pulls us down

Sometimes it feels unfair
The responsibilities in which we've been given
However we've inherited the role
We must not lose ourselves in it

Sometimes it feels scary
The not knowing what is to come
Yet trusting blindly with belief
The Universe always wants what's best for us

Sometimes if feels scarce
The funds are running low
With expenses building up
We struggle to be in abundant flow

Sometimes it feels lonely
The path in which we walk
When we want to connect with others
They are unable to truly support us

Sometimes it feels too heavy
The expectations we put on ourselves
When we can be more self-compassionate
The weight of the world we carry will begin to melt

Don't Suffer in Silence

Don't suffer in silence
Let your heart weep
Allow all that you've suppressed
To be heard and seen

Don't hesitate to ask for help
Knowing someone will always care
Let go of your worries of being judged
By others you meet out there

Through your courage and bravery
You may just be the light for another to see
Giving them the same permission
To reach out in their time of great need

Whatever your thoughts are
However they convince you to hide
No suffering you experience within
Is worth contemplating suicide

You are loved beyond measure
You matter to the depths of the sea
You are seen farther than the stars
You are one with Source Energy

Faces of Change

Change is a rhythm in which we find our own beat
It can often lift us high
Or bring us to our feet

Change invites us to lean into the discomfort
Its whispers are there
To wake us up

Change is where we get the opportunity to simply disrupt
Our patterns
Our fears
The thoughts in our mind where we get stuck

Change is the place where we can hear the music in our heart
And truly align
It is a canvas waiting to be painted
With new colors, textures and designs

Change is where we get to explore
Our purpose
Our path
Our passion
And so much more

So when change comes knocking at your door
Stay open and curious to what it brings
Welcome the gifts it holds for you
Be willing to gracefully receive

Though you may not know its purpose
And feel anxious when it greets you
Change is where you will discover
Your courage
Your capacity
Your deepest inner truth

Give permission to release your pain.
Or prohibit and be a prisoner of it.

No One Can Make You Feel

No one can make you feel
What doesn't already exist in you
That triggers your emotions deep
And awakens your unhealed wounds

No one can make you feel
Less than you are
Unless you give them the power
That belongs inside your own heart

No one can make you feel
Unworthy or unseen
If you yourself aren't able
To witness the value of your being

No one can make you feel
As if you are not smart
Because of the knowledge you share
Or the wisdom that you impart

No one can make you feel
What you don't feel is true
No matter the energy they project
Unconsciously upon you

No one can make you feel
What doesn't already exist in you
It's in how you choose to respond
That will keep you aligned to your truth

Misunderstood

There are going to be people
Who just do not get you
For reasons out of your control
Whatever is their trigger
Is simply not yours to own

There are going to be people who judge you
Through their own fears
But what they really struggle with most
Has nothing to do with you, my dear

You are just a mirror, a reflection
Of a deep wound they have not yet healed
So no matter what you do or say
You will be a projection of what they've unconsciously concealed

Of course it doesn't feel good
No human wants to feel rejected
For you to understand
Is look nowhere other than inward
For your own self-acceptance

You don't need to justify or prove
Your worthiness or brilliance
Merely hold compassion for the other
And recognize your inner resilience

So next time you feel misunderstood
Or you feel triggered inside
Take a moment to pause
And trust all that you are within
Is far purposeful and wise

Hold the Space

When you feel the pain
Don't resist
Simply hold the space
Let it sift

It needs to expand
And then contract
Don't hold it in
Don't hold back

Nurture it with love
Compassion and care
Let your pain know
You are there

Don't shame or fault
Don't judge or deny
Simply acknowledge its presence
Let it scream or cry

For your pain is seeking
Your acceptance and peace
All it wants
Is to be heard and seen

A Cry for Help

There is a cry for help
And it's showing its face
At the "broken" hands of mankind
Who is cut off from their own heart space

Let's silence the violence
By hearing loud and clear
That killing is never the answer
When one is in great despair

This world of form
We traverse each day
Holds so much unconsciousness
We can only pray

To awaken and rise higher
To see each other as whole
To hear the needs of each other
To connect soul to soul

Let's silence the violence
By reaching out our hand
Disarming our judgments and hatred
And contributing to making this a great land

No longer can we look the other way
And pretend we can't see
Just how disconnected we are
As a society

Though we cannot control
The choices and actions of others
We do hold the power within
To hold love and light for all our sisters and brothers

Our collective loving energy
Has the magnitude to change the heart
It can transform pain to purpose
It is a first step, a start

Let's silence the violence
By saying a prayer tonight
For those whose lives have been cut short
May they now be our guiding light

If You Knew Then

If you knew then
What you know now
Would you change anything
Or would you continue to allow

If so
What would it be
That you feel
Would have changed your life's trajectory

What would be the advice
You'd have given to your younger self
That would have given them permission
To look inward and nowhere else

How would you have held the space
For when their fears came up
What would you have done differently
To show them deeper self-love

Where would you have listened
With a more compassionate ear
Being less judgmental towards them
More open-hearted and ready to hear

What guidance would you offer
That could have liberated their soul
From carrying unnecessary weight
And empowering them to reach their goals

If you know now
What you didn't know then
Would you change anything
Or do it all the same again

Don't let a message of pain hurt you.
Instead allow the message to awaken your hurt and heal your pain.

Resistance and Acceptance

When you face adversity, when you feel defeated; remember everything you are and all you ever need is already seeded within your soul.

Look nowhere else but inside.

The Power of Resistance

When resistance shows its face
You are being asked to pay attention
To its fierce and piercing energy

At what speed is it coming toward you
In what direction is it going
To whom is it ricocheting off and reflecting onto

The force of its vibrations
Are relentless
Often ruthless

Its mission is to stop you in your tracks
And invite you to ask
What is this here to show me

If resistance is ignored
It will rage even louder
It will rattle the ground
Under your feet
It will bring you to your knees

Resistance makes a statement
It wants to be heard and seen
It will unconsciously get intertwined
And get buried underneath

The worry
The anxiety
The control
The fear

It will often show itself
As helplessness
And whisper in your ear

Don't let go
Hold onto me
I'll keep you in control
So you will always feel you 'know'

Unless you meet resistance with acceptance
It will seduce you to believe
That it has the power
Keeping you from what
You are truly meant to receive

Take a Deep Breath

Take a deep breath
And release
Ask yourself
What is it you need

What is arising
Within your soul
That is asking you
To simply let go

Where are you feeling
The depths of your pain
How is it showing itself
Over and over again

What is the story
You're telling yourself
That keeps you safe
From asking for help

Who are you
Underneath your "mask"
When will you surrender
Your tight-fisted grasp

If you dare to live
Brave and bold
What would be the new story
That would be told

How would you feel then
Knowing you're free
Choosing a life of liberation
Then living in perhaps misery

Take a deep breath
And allow
The truth of your being
To meet the moment of now

When I let go of my story,
I discover a new beginning.

Break Through Your Own Walls

Are you truly listening
To what is being said
Are you hearing from your heart
Or resisting from your head

So many times
You think instead of feel
You often miss the message
That is calling you to heal

The story you are saying
And unconsciously believe
Keeps you from accepting
All that you are meant to receive

So long as you stay comfortable
And justify your ways
The Universe will move along
Trusting where you are is "okay"

Dare to disrupt your patterns
Break through your own walls
Start listening with curiosity
Be willing to embrace the fall

In that process of growth
Your ability to listen will deepen
It will allow you to hear clearly
The divine answers within

And when you rise up
You will begin to see
Your inner truth expands
Like branches from a tree

They will reach out
Far and wide
Connecting you to others
Where you can no longer deny or hide

Wonder

There is so much wonder for you to receive
In the daily awakening of your life
Only when you allow yourself to believe
You are whole, worthy and divine

Whatever you put your heart to
However the effort you make
Will the opportunities then come through
To discover, lean into and take

The only limits that exist
Are the conversations in your mind
That you often suppress and resist
Creating false beliefs of "falling behind"

From where you think you should be
Or how much money you are to earn
Based on what others perceive or see
As a measurement of your self-worth

The world is your oyster
There are many jewels in the sea
The ocean is vast and a mirror
Of allowing your soul to be set free

Let the tides take you high
And the waves ride you slow
Let the stillness of the water
Be a compass to all that you already know

There is so much wonder for you to receive
In the daily awakening of your life
Only when you allow yourself to achieve
What you came here for in this life

Traversing the Daily Challenges

I'm right there with you
No greater no less
Traversing the daily challenges
And doing my damn best

You can bet I've screwed up
Said many unconscious things
Projected my lack
And acted childishly

Have I beaten myself up
And sulked hours in guilt
Indeed so and many days
I've just wanted to wilt

But that process only works
For a small period of time
Before the real waking up happens
Calling my spirit to align

To the deeper root cause
That I am experiencing inside
Learning from my mistakes
And not indulging my pride

Yet if I chose
To stay asleep at the wheel
Travel the road of resistance
Then suffer I will feel

I will make mistakes
I will rise and fall
Yet the truth of my existence
Is when I accept myself for all

I have found the gold
When I silence the mind
When I nurture my being
And allow grace by my side

I am human
I am soul
I am wisdom
I am whole

Don't look in the rearview mirror of fear.
Rather look ahead through the lens of love.

Lack and Abundance

The burden and the blessing

The pain and the possibility

The opposition and the opportunity

The lecture and the lesson

The failure and the fortune

The tribulation and the triumph

*...for it is through the lens of what you see
that you will be.*

You Always Have a Choice

Have gratitude when you clean
For the foundation and structure
That holds you up
Where you live and breathe

And even when you see the mess
Take a pause
And remind yourself
Many others live with far less

While it may feel like a chore
Sweeping and dusting away
Cleaning toilets and sinks
Fear of missing out or feeling bored

Yet you always have a choice
In how you view your life
Complaining and whining
Or use the cleaning space to empower your inner voice

Pay attention to your thoughts
That are moving in that physical space
While you declutter and rid the dirt
What do you find inside coming up

Feel grateful for all you own
Take pride and respect in it
Feel the energy around you
Cleanse the inner spaces you call home

Perspective

All of life is a perspective
From the lens in which we see
Life happening for you
Or life happening "to me"

When the days flow with ease
We seldom stop and blink
Going about it casually
Until life is on a brink

Then we shift our mindset
From a place of love to fear
We may begin to feel unsettled
And need to take a hard look in the mirror

What is this here to teach me
How can I grow from my pain
Where is this meant to steer me
So I can find the ways in which to change

The way we are called to grow
Is often out of our hands
Rather through the obstacles in life
That allow us to better understand

All of life is a perspective
From the lens in which we see
Life is not here
To make things so easy

Life is going to push
Life is going to pull
Life is a playground
To get you closer to your soul

Your Story is a Reflection

Your story is a reflection
Of what you are resisting inside
The power of its mirror
Will not allow you to hide

The script will be seductive
It will make you believe all you think is true
You will unconsciously manipulate the words
To avoid feeling the pain come through

Your story is a protection
Of justifying your fears
The armor of its cover
Will inhibit your ability to hear

It will shout out through the ego
Drowning the whispers of your heart
Tell you it's not okay to cry
When you feel the need to fall apart

It will keep showing its face
Until you finally see
What pages need to be removed
So you can live more authentically

Your story is a reflection
Of the power you hold inside
And the choices you make in telling it
Will only liberate your mind

Divorce your shadow. Marry your light.

Yearning to Break Free

Our mind is …

A construction built to believe, to do, to think
That our thoughts create a gross false identity
Obscuring us from our truest being

A playground designed for our ego to run rampant and free
Where temper tantrums seek shelter
Displaying our inner lack, wants and needs

A courthouse where judgment is held
Where stories and lies are told
Cases being made to compel
Contaminating the root of our soul

A template designed to make us believe
Our own delusion
Which only causes us nothing
More than inner confusion

Contained by conditions
Power and greed
Longing to be heard
Validated and seen

Infant in its unfolding
Seeking guidance through its own maze
Searching for the light within
Yet often in a mere daze

Armored for combat
Believing it's right
Willing to risk itself
In any given fight

Imprisoned by thought
Sanctioned by belief
Wrapped in seduction
Yearning to break-free

The mind finally begins to surrender control
When it hears the whisper of *the spirit*
Inviting it to let go

Come sit with me and release your fears
That you have held onto for too many years
It's time to connect to the Divine within you
Break down the walls that have been suppressing your truth
You are now forever free
To just be

A Few Doors Down

Do you think the grass is greener
A few doors down
Because they have a fancier car
Or a much bigger house

Do you think you're the only one
Who wishes for a different life
Just because you don't hear others
Talk out loud about their strife

Do you think the millionaire
Is far more successful than you
Because society measures wealth
Not on who you are but what you do

Do you think the famous
Are immune to their own fears
Because the media determines
What you will or will not hear

Do you think your children
"Should" do as you say
Because you are the adult
Who was once too raised this way

Do you think your feelings
Aren't worthy to be heard
Because you were told it's weak
To show others when you're hurt

Do you think your dreams
Are just a figment in your mind
Because the possibility of realizing them
Won't happen in this lifetime

Do you think too much
To the point it brings you down
Only when you stop the thoughts
Can the truth of your soul be found

As We Look Ahead

As we look ahead
To another year
May we embrace more love
And disengage from our fears

May we keep our arms wide open
Along with our hearts and eyes
May we receive what comes our way
Seeing it as a blessing in disguise

May we let go of what doesn't serve us
And only allow what does
May we be steadfast in our journey
Trusting the path that we are on

May we be easy on ourselves
When our thoughts steer a different way
May we recognize that making changes
Does not happen in one day

As we look ahead
To another year
May be more self-compassionate
And connect deeper to the inner whispers we hear

Thank you, Universe, for showing me what
I most need to learn today.

I am open to receiving the lessons with
gratitude and acceptance.

Life and Loss

The power of one's presence in another's moment of pain, is the portal to creating greater empathy and compassion in our world.

What Our Life Is All About

We may not really understand
What our life is all about
As we walk the peaks and valleys
And make our way throughout

Some days we will stumble
Other days we will simply fall
It's in how we choose to get up
That will empower us to heed the call

A positive mindset is one part
To forging the path ahead
But if we don't feel it deep in our bones
We may take many wrong turns instead

And in those times of despair
Can we then begin to see
That our life here on earth
Isn't meant to be lived out "perfectly"

We are here to explore
We are here to create
We are here to experience
We are here to appreciate

The lessons we've come to learn
The gifts we've come to impart
The past we've come to heal
So we can honor the truth of our heart

Baylie

An angel named Baylie
Who came here to be
To spread her love
And shine so brightly

Has been called back to her heavenly home
Leaving so many loved ones here on earth
With a piece of her presence
That will forever be cherished

The impact she made
The lives she changed
The purpose she was called to serve
Holds depths of beauty
In this time of deep pain

Through the fight of her life
Her soul spoke to each of us
No matter the distance
We came together as one

So when we feel a tug
Or hear a whisper in our ear
We will know that she is one of our angels above
Now guiding us down here

There Are No Words

There are no words
Only faith
When a mother is praying for her child to wake

There are no words
Only light
When a mother is feeling deep pain at night

There are no words
Only love
When a mother misses her child so much

There are no words
Only hope
When a mother is desperate to know

There are no words
Only now
When a mother begs to understand how

There are no words
Only peace
When a mother is being asked to surrender and release

There are no words
Only trust
When a mother is raising her hands to the angels above

There are no words
Only community
That comes together far and wide during a mother's aching need

May we all continue to unite
Spread our prayers
And healing light

May we hold the beloved in our hearts
Wrap our collective wings around them tight
Knowing they are giving everything they've got
To fight this fight

Incarnation

Long before this physical form
We've lived many past lives
Bringing us to the here and now
So we could see with our own eyes

How we choose this life
To experience its beauty and pain
Through the mind, body and soul
We get this opportunity to co-create

Our path to freedom
Our freedom to choose
Love over fear
In all that we do

Yet "the story" we carry
Along the way
Strongly hinders us
Leading us astray

We can get off track
And struggle to find
Our purpose for this incarnation
Because we've been living too much from our mind

But if we remember
The soul contract we made
Before we came to earth
We will live from that whole integrated place

Trying to Make Sense

Life may be going
According to "plan"
And just like that
You can't understand

How one moment
All is well
And the next moment
Can feel like complete hell

Trying to make sense
Or find reason or rhyme
Will cause you deep distress
Every single time

This doesn't imply
You dismiss how you feel
Express your emotions
Allow yourself to be real

Then release and trust
There is a reason for it
While you can't see it now
Underneath the pain is a gift

Hold it sacred
Embrace with love
Your angels are guiding you
Always from above

Life may be going
According to "plan"
Detach from the outcome
So you can receive with and open heart and hand

Life in This Physical Form

Life in this physical form
Is one that we often take for granted
It carries us through so much
Yet we unconsciously turn our back on it

We expect so much from our body
Pushing and demanding it heeds
Seldom do we stop and ask
What is it that you (my body) needs

Quietude and peace
Perhaps rest and repair
Detoxification of toxins
Or maybe nourishment and self-care

Think of the burden it holds
From many generations past
Our body isn't made of stone
Nor was it built to forever last

There was unfinished business elsewhere
In one or many of our past lives
That needed this physical mind and body
To heal and reckon its pain in this lifetime

Life in this physical form
Was created to help us grow
For it is we who incarnated into this body
Just as our spirit called us so

We are all vessels flowing with the current of life.

The Day I Died

Once upon a time on that January day
I experienced a severe car crash
That changed my fate

Heading home from work
After a long busy day
I made a U-turn
In front of my place

When I began my turn
I had not seen the car
In a blink of an eye
I was in the ER

Ruptured bladder
Punctured lungs
Fractured pelvis
Five broken ribs

My two-week stay in the hospital
Had just begun

My cheerleading days were over
Though I kept hope to make the team
A new life awaited me
At the age of seventeen

I had to learn some of the basics
All over again
Hooked to a catheter
Felt like the pain would never end

I was surrounded by deep love
Showered with incredible support
Considering the depth of my injuries
My healing time was rather short

I often feel
As if that day a part of me died
Unconscious to my own mind
That instead allowed my body to survive

Knowing what I now know
I can see it wasn't my time
For *The Universe* had its own plan
Along with its guiding angels by my side

Simply Release

The closing of another year
Draws near

Reflections of days past
Gone fast

What once felt so surreal
Is now real

We realize the truth
That it was not meant to last

The days are borrowed
Through joy and sorrow

To help us grow
In ways we can't always know

And when those days are gone
They must simply move on

So we can continue to learn the lessons
And unfold

Do not fret or fear
As we bid farewell to another year
Instead give thanks and hold grace

Take a moment to pause
For each year holds its own cause
Giving us the gift to expand our heart space

Look back with peace
Look ahead with purpose
Trust *The Universe*

Simply release
To let the truth of you rise and be

Love Is

Love is sometimes yes
It is sometimes no
Love has boundaries
When it feels messy and out of control

Love is not linear
It's not logical or straight
Love can move mountains
In the force of hate

Love is abstract
It is a vibrational wave
Love is a feeling
Not everyone feels it the same

Love is boundless
It has no end
Love brings people together
It helps hearts mend

Love is a balance
When there is pain
Love is not meant
To be held in vain

Love is a container
It holds us safe
Love allows our emotions
To be seen and embraced

Love is neutral
It is pure and real
Love is the face of a child
Its beauty can be surreal

Love doesn't judge
It does not condemn
Love is not an enemy
It is an energy to befriend

Love has no color
It is brilliant and bright
Love can be blinding
It can awaken the night

Love is an action
Its energy is magnetic
Love beats inside of us
Its vibration is electric

Love is cellular
It is one with our soul
Love is a seed
That blossoms and grows

Love holds the power
It can transform and heal
Love is medicinal
When we allow ourselves to feel

Love is a vessel
It flows through each breath
Love is an angel
Guiding each life and death

Love is you
It is me
Love is one
With Source Energy

The World Is a Stage

The world is a stage
For all to see
The gifts we've all come to share
To strengthen our humanity

And just like a Broadway production
There are many moving parts
Each lending a helping hand
To touch a billion hearts

We've all got a purpose
That plays a vital role
To unify our humanness
While honoring our soul

Evolution is a process
That doesn't happen overnight
It often comes through trial and error
Before we can try to "get it right"

Each person will arrive
In their due time
There is no race to self-growth
And definitely no finish line

We will cycle many lives over
To learn what we are called to
The choice is always in our hands
For how we wish to navigate through

The world is a stage
For each of us to be
The truth of ourselves
To live whole and free

Don't abandon yourself when your feelings need you most.

Being and Doing

*I will not let my thoughts swallow me or drown my
dreams, for my breath is the air that so
lovingly carries me.*

It gives me oxygen and is food to my soul.

I am more than my thoughts; I am whole.

I Cannot Help But See

Everywhere I go
I cannot help but see
How many people
Are living in misery

Completely disconnected
From their own heart
Yet seeking wholeness
From others' "broken" parts

We didn't get here
Overnight you know
It's been gradually building
As more are feeling alone

Technology has severed
The very life line in our soul
Keeping our heads facing down
Everywhere we go

We then get lost
In the social media fantasy
Believing false truths
Living through others vicariously

It's truly disheartening
To say the very least
How technology has intoxicated us
And we keep feeding the beast

But we always have a choice
In the way we engage
That of true human connection
Or virtually run away

So start to look around
Pay attention to all the pain
Change only happens
When we begin to change our ways

Release the Need to Be

Where are you rushing to
What do you feel you'll miss
Are you feeling left out
Watching others "accomplish"

Whose timetable are you on
What scale are you measuring against
How exhausted do you feel
Upon your day's rest

The pressure you endure
The stress you imbibe
Is it truly worth it all
As you take inventory of your life

What moments are you wishing
You had captured more in your day
How can you empower yourself differently
To create a more harmonious way

Release the need to be
Anyone than who you are
No one is designed like you
So go shine your own bright star

Time

The minutes pass more quickly
By the hurried feelings of the day
Before we know it we're wondering
How we've lost track of time then complain

What we don't really understand
As our minds are too minuscule
That time is infinite and abundant
It's a choice of burning through it or helping us to fuel

We are the ones who hold the key
To how we drive our day
At every intersection of our life
We get to decide yay or nay

Time doesn't berate us
If we took more of it or used less
Time is merely a continuum
That shows up for us regardless

We've all wasted time on things
That have held little to no regard
And other moments we've embraced time
Holding it so closely we didn't want to part

As we walk our journey each day
We must do it hand in hand with time
Having gratitude for its limitless space
So we can stay connected to the divine

Just as with each new season
Brings about a bolstering bloom
Does time rebirth and replenish
So we too can rediscover and redo

The Ways of The World

We are all so consumed
By the ways of the world
We are juggling a thousand things at once
Our heads are in a swirl

The moment we wake up
We reach for our phones
Don't want to miss out
Don't want to feel alone

From getting the kids ready
Packing lunches for school
Rushing out the door
Eating breakfast in carpool

The madness gets worse
When we take to the roads
Distracted drivers everywhere
Makes us angry and cold

We hustle and we bustle
For what and for why
We're driving ourselves crazy
Often feeling like we're doing "to die"

The stresses we co-create
In any given day
Is setting no good example
On teaching our kids how to live a better way

Keeping up with the Joneses
Outdoing the other in form
It's no wonder our children
Feel the need to conform

Yet we are so oblivious
To the part we play
We victimize ourselves
We have no time in the day

We blame and we pity
Woe is me
What we are missing
Is our inability to choose wisely

We have the power
In each moment of the day
To rise more readily
And face what comes our way

We can make the shift
If we are truly willing to grow
And stop making excuses
And going with the flow

Sure life is busy
And yes at times hard
But we all have a story
That can keep us barred

Being open to change
And showing up for you
Is the only real decision
That you have to commit to

Permission to Feel

It's a process to unravel
All that you've known
Conditioned behaviors at the root
From what your life has currently shown

Go easy on yourself
As you lean into the discomfort
Expect there to be some uproar
No guarantee it's going to be pleasant

Is the cost higher
To stay where you are
Or to chance new beginnings
That can take you more far

Create the space
To evaluate your life
It's the best gift you can give yourself
In this moment in time

From your place of despair, you are being
called to rise and repair.

Pause

Too much noise goes on in our heads
Every second of the day
Combined with the external noise
We are filled with anxiety in every way

The "shoulda", "coulda" and "woulda" syndrome
That spirals us further down the hole
Creates deeper triggers and reactions
Distancing us from true connection in our home

We all want to be heard and seen
And know that what we say matters
Yet not enough do we pause to feel what is going on inside
Rather we seek acceptance from the other

How are we feeling in any given moment
What is the need that can only be met by us
Where are we projecting outwardly to serve our own story
What is at the root of our own inner stress

It is only when we get silent
Can we hear the truth within
Even though we may feel deeply resistant
That is how true healing begins

The power of a pause
Speaks louder than any spoken word
And in that moment we just "sit with it"
Are we all ever truly heard

Detach from The Outcome

Detach from the outcome
To lessen your suffering and pain
When you release the grip on your life
Your hands will remain more open to gain

Pain is a path you must take to grow
For if you avoid or resist
You will miss its divine purpose
Which holds the beauty and the gift

When you feel in lack
It's a mirror that is asking you to see
How you can change your vibration higher
And redirect your energy

Life isn't meant to unfold
According to your agenda or plans
Rather *The Universe* guides you gracefully
Reminding you it always has your back

Choosing to Disconnect

There's a reason I don't watch the news
Because it breeds anxiety and fear
I consciously made this decision
When my daughter approached her first year

Have I "missed out" on the world happenings
Perhaps to some degree yes
But looking at what I've truly gained by being disconnected
I'd say has been for the best

While time itself is a commodity
And I rarely capture its full worth
I believe we must often make choices
That best serve us first

Get curious
Ask questions
Observe your patterns
And witness how you are showing up

Where are you giving your power away
Sit with all before you to see
How the outside world can zap your energy

Choose differently
Empower your being
Nurture your soul's heart
Even if it means you have to stand apart

No Barriers

It is in the space and time
that our energy expands and breathes
with no barriers

It is in the silence and stillness
that our heart listens and feels
with no conditions

It is in the attuning and discerning
that our wisdom rises and guides
with no questions

It is in the breakdown and breakthrough
that our pain releases and heals
with no sorrow

It is in the here and now
that our presence arrives and receives
with no resistance

It is in the surrender and trust
that our mind knows and allows
with no control

Anxiety

Anxiety is irrational
It doesn't understand
It wants what it wants
It wants it on command

Anxiety is a beast
It seeks to be fed
It will trick you to believe
It will screw with your head

Anxiety is a loop
It will cycle like a wheel
It doesn't know fact from fiction
It believes its needs are real

Anxiety is a prison
It will keep you locked behind
It will inhibit you from living
It will try to take over your mind

Anxiety is excessive
It will run you day and night
It has no regard for others
It will instigate and fight

Anxiety is a trigger
It can set off a false alarm
It doesn't know the difference
It thinks all things will harm

Anxiety is an intruder
It steals your comfort and joy
It leaves you feeling empty
It can affect the youngest girl or boy

Anxiety is a maze
It will find its way out
It doesn't matter the circumstance
It causes so much confusion and doubt

Anxiety is deaf
It is unable to decipher and hear
It misfires signals in the body
It causes hypervigilance and fear

Anxiety is a necessary evil
It can protect us from danger
It can keep us highly alert
It acts as a patrolling ranger

Anxiety is ancestral
It runs generations deep
It can show up at anytime
It can wake us from our sleep

Anxiety is exhausting
It can rob your energy
It can manifest in multiple ways
It can be experienced so differently

Retreat

What is that feeling inside
That is trying to be known
To take you from your place of doubt
As you scroll through the feed on your phone

How often do you schedule a date
To be completely by yourself
To hear the whispers of your soul
With no disruptions from anyone else

Where is that special place you go
To get away from it all
That is only yours to know
And heed your highest call

Who is - if any - that one person
You trust to share your heart
No worries of being judged
When you feel the need to come apart

See we spend so much time
And much of our energy
Doing for the other
Often neglecting our own being

In the hustle and bustle of life
We need to pause and see
It's crucial for our own health
To go within ourselves and retreat

Let Go and Let Flow

This day has found
Its own flow
Unbeknownst to me
One to simply let go

Though calls were scheduled
And the to-do list was outlined
The Universe invited me instead to pause
And surrender the pressures of my mind

One to simply be
To release the expectations
To feel the presence of my heart
And embrace all its sensations

To connect to my soul
To hold the sacred space
To sit contentedly alone
To receive with trust and grace

To shed a few tears
To hug someone new
To nurture my fears
To feel my way through

To surrender to the unknown
To witness my mind
To hear the music playing
Deep within me inside

So if for only this moment
I was called to pause from what I had planned
To stop the doing and embrace the being
Then received this gift I have from *The Universe's* hand

For the only moment that truly matters
Is in the moment of now
Where I am one with my breath
As I simply just allow

When you find yourself in a power struggle,
raise your energetic vibration.

It will change the frequency between
your connection.

Difference and Oneness

The more you peel back the layers of your conditioning,
the more you reveal the gifts within.

The Way We Are Wired

Though we all come
From Source Energy
The way we are wired
Is very unique

From our personality traits
To the way we think
What matters to you
May not matter to me

From the way we are driven
To the way we feel
What may seem senseless to you
May be something I believe to be real

From the way we process
To the way we speak
What you find boring
May be of most interest to me

From our own inner compass
To our specific heart and will
What I may be for another
May require you to just be still

From the way we make decisions
To the way we take action
What I may need to feel satisfied
May invite you to just see what happens

From how we store our fears
To how we survive
What I may find therapeutic
May require different of you to feel alive

From the way we handle pressure
To the way we feel secure
What I may need to feel that rush
Might be simply too much for you to endure

Yet knowing how different
We all truly are
Somehow we create systems
That push us too far

They put us in a box
Asking us to be the same
Only to come find out
"The system" is its own game

We are not all meant
To produce alike
We have all been designed
To share our individual qualities of life

So don't try to be
Someone you're not
You will only feel frustrated
And get more tangled in a knot

Keep discovering who you are
Go deeper than before
Allow all of who you are
To walk the path that is only yours

When we can appreciate
Each other's beautiful flare
Will we unite more freely
As we breathe the same air

Though we all come
From Source Energy
The way we are wired
Is so on purpose for all to see

Stop Judging

Stop judging…

Those who do not fancy up their hair just right
Who do not dress in "fashion"
Who struggle to keep their house clean
Whose body isn't "fit"
Who is losing sleep at night

Stop judging, start empathizing
Stop gossiping, start empowering
Stop shaming, start engaging

Stop judging…

Those who struggle to know their own worth
Who desire to be seen and accepted
Who are afraid to speak of their pain
Who fear it will only cause greater hurt

Stop judging, start accepting
Stop gossiping, start communicating
Stop shaming, start supporting

Stop judging…

Those who have a child with "more needs"
Who does not enroll their child in every sport
Whose child isn't at the top of their class
Who is not pressuring their child to go to an Ivy League

Stop judging, start loving
Stop gossiping, start learning
Stop shaming, start listening

Stop judging…

Those whose partnership is not "ideal"
Who struggles to pay the bills
Who is living a false life
Who longs to feel more "real"

Stop judging, start feeling
Stop gossiping, start bonding
Stop shaming, start being

Available
Compassionate
Curious
Understanding
Authentic
Silent
Open
Community

When we create the vibrational energy amongst each other, we
expand our frequency waves to nourish our collective spirit

We open our hearts wider and our children feel the love,
acceptance and worthiness to an even greater degree

Our lives feel richer no matter how much money we have in the bank

Our capacity to rise and lead through the uncharted waters of our
personal and parental unfolding seems limitless and within reach

We are one no better than the other

We are all warriors at heart desiring the very
best for ourselves and families

We must be able to lean on each other and lean into the
discomfort knowing judgment doesn't seep into those cracks

Instead, we must be the light to help each along the way

The freedom that comes through self-expression
overpowers any judgement cast by another.

From the Same Energy

I am different from you
You are different from me
Yet we are the same in many ways
Experiencing life as human beings

We each have our own unique traits
That may often seem that we are alike
Our difference is within our respective spirits
And how we came to express them in this life

It is only when we get mired
In our own minds
That we begin to construct labels and judgments
Which ultimately create a divide

Our hearts from each other
Our hands from service
Our eyes from seeing
There may be difference yet equally oneness

The Struggle

Please don't judge a child
When you see them acting out
For you may not really understand
What it is all about

While they appear "normal"
As can be
Doesn't mean they aren't struggling
With something internally

Far too often we assume
A child is "bad"
When we see them tantrum
Believing the parent is raising a "brat"

Instead allow your ego to cast aside
And begin to wonder
How the parent and child
Must really be feeling inside

No child deliberately plans
To scream and make a scene
Many times it is out of their own inability
To feel calm and at ease

We all must be more understanding
Empathetic and compassionate
And put ourselves in their place
Asking how would we handle it

We have all been there
In some time of our own
When everyone is staring at us
Have we not truly feel alone

A child who has "more needs"
May have them in a way it can't been seen
But it doesn't lessen the challenge
Of their reality

The last thing anyone wants is to feel judged
So the next time you see a child tantrum
Or a parent feeling helpless
Extend to them both a warm smile or hug

Equal

No matter the teachings I ingest
Or the clients in which I coach
I'm equally one on this journey
To rise higher and experience deep growth

No matter "if I feel I know better"
Or the guilt brings me down
I'm willing to take responsibility
To learn better the next time around

No matter how many books I've read
Or classes that I've taken
I'm a constant student of life
To understand the power of my co-creation

No matter what others expect
Or their perception of who I am to be
I'm the only one who truly matters
To stay in my truth and authenticity

No matter where I was before
Or where my path continues to go
I'm allowing myself to be and feel human
To love and accept myself as whole

No Longer Comparing

Does it appear others are doing "more"
Than what seems to be for you
And getting disillusioned by it
Feeling as if you have something to prove

To view your life from this lens
Will limit and keep you feeling "small"
For where they are and where you are
There is no comparison at all

Who you are here to be
Is unique in your own way
To allow yourself to think you are "lesser than"
Will cause your own vibrational decay

The mind is oh so sneaky
It wants you to believe
That others are "greater than"
Therefore you are "not worthy" to receive

If you should find you are seduced
By such egoic lies
Place your hand upon your heart
And gently close your eyes

Listen for the whisper
Deep within your soul
The one that is the only truth
That is meant for you to behold

Then emanate from that space
Where your energy feels light
Releasing all that no longer serves you
And embodying only what feels "right"

This is how we grow
Into our higher self
No longer comparing or desiring to be
Anywhere or anyone else

Friends

We start early on believing
Everyone is our friend
We give pieces of our heart
We innocently let them in

We go about life
Adding more friends along the way
Not truly realizing not every friend
Is here to stay

If we think of friends
As we do the many seasons
We will realize early on
Each one serves a specific reason

Some come to us
At a time of great need
Holding the space with compassion
As we cry aloud and release

Some come to us
To show where we need to grow
Reflecting those places within
That we have yet to discover and know

Some come to us
They bring out our best
Passing time in laughter
To be more laid back with less stress

Whomever the friend
Wherever you go
The one friend for life
Is the one within your soul

It will never let you down
It will expect nothing in return
It will hold you safe for life
It will be there to help you learn

Who you truly are
Who you are meant to be
The friend within your soul
Is one for eternity

There Will Be Many Who Disagree

There will be many who disagree
With the choices that you make
They will impose their opinions
Feeling entitled by what they have to say

You can take the higher road
And choose to send them light
Or you can waste your time and energy
Trying to prove who is "wrong or right"

The child within you
Wants to rant
Protect itself
And fight back

The adult self
Knows wiser
Takes a pause
And rises higher

So hard to find the balance
In that given moment
This is when tapping into your truth
Will teach you how to flow with it

And only then can you hear
What the other is trying to say
It has more to do with them
Then about the choices that you make

Not a One Size Fits All

Yes we are one
But not a one size fits all
Though we come from the same *Universe*
We are each designed for a specific purpose and call

The human species
Has evolved tremendously over time
Where once we survived on pure instincts
Now we have been conditioned to live through our mind

And once again
We are on the precipice of change
The hierarchy of institutions
Is no longer the way

We are seeing more power
Rising in women and children alike
Dictatorship of men as it once was
No longer will suffice

Our awareness is expanding
Far greater and wide
For humanity as a whole
Is preparing for the turn of the tide

We are becoming more one with ourselves
Constant discovery of the truth
That's been buried behind
And time to uproot

Let not these shifts
Cause fear or concern
It's only when the Phoenix rises
That something must burn

*Freedom and liberation come when we release the
need to look externally for validation,
acceptance and approval.*

*Freedom invites us instead to focus
only in one direction.*

Inward.

Truth and Beliefs

*The truth unfolds when you let go of
the story being told.*

Release of Limiting Beliefs

As the Full Moon is here
It is an opportunity for us to clear
All that is taking space in our mind
That is not serving, loving or kind

And so we are given this chance
To create a new intimate dance
One where we can flow
Allowing us to cleanse and let go

Close your eyes and feel
What is heavy and not real
Release it out from within
Let it be carried away by the wind

Now put your hand on your heart
Hold compassion as you start
Breathing in new energy and peace
Affirm your wholeness through this sacred release

Vibrations of The Inner Voice

Your inner voice is a vibration
It resounds loud and strong
And when you align to your knowing
Will you trust it is never wrong

Your inner voice is a symphony
It plays many beautiful tunes
And when you listen carefully
Will you hear its deepest truth

It is trusting your wisdom
Even when others question your words
It is believing your heart
Even when others may feel hurt

It is holding your ground
Even when others step on your feet
It is awakening your spirit
Even when others are asleep

It is heeding your calling
Even when others resist your purpose
It is shining your light
Even when others are still searching

It is feeling your presence
Even when others block your energy
It is owning your power
Even when others push your boundaries

It is quieting your mind
Even when others control the noise
It is knowing your truth
Even when others make a different choice

We've Lost Our Way

We live in a world
Where we struggle to feel real
Where we long to know our truth
Where we find ourselves lost and confused

Because we've listened
For far too long
To what everyone else thinks
To what everyone else wants for us

We've lost our way
Caring more of what people have to say
Then trusting our inner voice
Allowing that to lead the way

No wonder
People are overmedicating
Filled with anxieties
Running scared and afraid

Buying more than they need
Living unauthentically
Wondering how to escape
From all their inner pain

Searching for hope
Looking for answers
Begging to be seen and heard
For who it is they truly are

The real war is going on inside of us
The real battleground is where we stand in this moment
The real need is to connect to our inner child
Giving them what they never got long ago

Only when we break those walls that divide our own heart
Can we then begin to set ourselves free
Only when we stop seeking external approval
Can we live authentically

Breaking Patterns

Breaking patterns can be so hard
For they require you to really see
How you co-create the dynamics
That cause the unfolding of its complexities

Patterns are created through fear
They are a way to keep you safe
For when you feel helpless
You control your feelings from this knowing place

Breaking patterns requires disruption
From the cycle of repetition
It will cause an uproar no doubt
Especially when it meets its competition

Patterns are built over time
They get bigger and stronger with force
The more you feed them attention
The less you choose "better" and instead ignore

Breaking patterns will bring out the tears
You may find yourself on your knees
For anytime you are changing habits
It will cause you great unease

Patterns carry an energy
That can pulsate through your being
If you aren't attuned to its intentions
You will mistake its purpose and reasoning

Breaking patterns help you expand
Your heart and your soul
When you learn to surrender and allow
The need for patterns will be no more

WHO you truly are

WHAT you have to offer the world

*WHEN you are in alignment
with your truth*

*WHERE you surrender and trust
The Universe*

HOW you share your voice

Is …

WHY you are here.

Being in Your Truth

When you feel naked and bare
When you can look yourself in the mirror
When you truly don't have a care
When you take a leap and dare
That is being in your truth

As you feel the unease
As you fall to your knees
As you let go of the need to please
As you create deep inner peace
That is being in your truth

Allowing your heart space to expand
Allowing your inner voice to demand
Allowing your feet to take a stand
Allowing your hand to take another's hand
That is being in your truth

Having the courage to rise
Having the strength inside
Having the will to survive
Having the power to stay wise
That is being in your truth

When you feel lighter and free
When you find it's easier to breathe
When you can simply be
When you can say *I accept me*
That is being in your truth

Not an Enemy

Release the mind
From its role
From running your life
And wanting to be in control

The mind never asked
To carry this much weight
Its purpose isn't here
To decide your fate

The mind is a portal
That processes your thoughts
That filters ideas and concepts
From inspirations its brought

Somewhere you were told
And mistakenly taught
That your mind is your authority
To getting what you want

Just put your mind to it
And you'll figure it out
Weigh out all your options
And you should have less doubt

Yet here we all are
In the same time and place
Relying on our mind
To get us through life's "rat race"

It isn't our mind
That is the one to decide
Rather our innate body intelligence
Where we trust the truth as our guide

Release the mind
Set it free to be
That of an ally
And not an "enemy"

Vortex of Your Thoughts

The vortex of your thoughts
Can spiral you out of control
They can swallow you up
And have a hold on your throat

They can limit your freedom
And keep you standing still
The vortex of your thoughts
Can steer your dreams quickly downhill

When your thoughts arise
You always have a choice
Let them pass through you "as is"
Or give it an empowered voice

See your thoughts want attention
And will be persistent until you give in
They will often do what they need to
To ensure they always win

Yet the true power lies within you
Each and every time
Asking *how does this thought best serve me*
As it begins to enter your mind

Recognize it's only energy
It's not tangible or real
The vortex of your thoughts
Exist merely so you can begin to heal

Those inner wounds
Those unmet needs
Those dormant feelings
That all need room to breathe

So allow the energy to move through you
Be present with all that comes up
Don't judge or criticize the beautiful existence
Of the vortex of your thoughts

Life happens.
Feelings arise.
Emotions emit.
Choose wisely.
Be real.
Connect within.
Breathe deeply.
Express authentically.
Detach bravely.
Release freely.
Trust intuitively.
Accept lovingly.
Believe knowingly.
Truth transcends.

Boundaries

Boundaries are sacred
And necessary for your evolution
They will inevitably cause discomfort
To another who simply refuses them

Boundaries are not meant to divide
Or cause upheaval and strife
They are merely meant to create clarity
And communicate where you draw the line

Boundaries may appear harsh
Depending on the nature of its need
Yet when created with great awareness
They align with your inner truth and divinity

Boundaries are a language
That lets the other know
What you will accept
And when you've chosen to say no

Boundaries are a friend
That keep you honest and true
They hold you responsible
To being the most authentic you

Boundaries are not barriers
Or walls of steel
They are bridges connecting to your heart
So it can find peace as it heals

Boundaries take courage
They require knowing and self-worth
It takes practice and persistence
To see them "at work"

Go easy on yourself
Be patient with the process
Each unfolding moment
Is here to teach us

Where can you speak up more
Or perhaps speak less
How can creating a boundary
Allow you to rise to your highest self

When It No Longer Feels Right

When it no longer feels right
Release and surrender
Don't hold on so tight

When it no longer feels real
Trust that knowing
So you can honor and heal

When it no longer feels true
Have grace and compassion
For being in your truth

When it no longer feels safe
Leave the situation
And find a new place

When it no longer feels best
Appreciate what you've gathered
And let go of the rest

When it no longer feels aligned
Steer your path in a new direction
Knowing there is something new to find

Conversations of The Heart

What conversation are you afraid to have
That may affect how others feel
Are you concerned they will be mad
More than being in your truth and speaking what is real

The more you suppress
And hold inside
The feelings you are feeling
Because of fear or pride

You deny your inner child
Their voice to be heard
So they start to believe this as their truth
And lose their sense of worth

They dim their light
And hide their tears
Allowing others to shine more bright
Protecting their heart that they cannot hear

The whispers within
That are resonating in their soul
Calling them to awaken
To trust and to know

What they have to offer
What they have to say
Has deep meaning and purpose
In every single way

So when you doubt or wonder
If you should have that conversation
Take a moment to check-in
For you never know if they can make a lasting impression

I am my most authentic self when
I serve my truth and purpose.

Parent and Child

Rather than asking your child what they want to be when they grow up, encourage them to be enough just as they are. Divine in their wholeness and worthiness.

Parenting Isn't a Destination

I will say the "wrong" things
And get triggered in a flash
No matter how much inner work I do
It doesn't exempt me not to react

I can hold guilt and shame
And sulk in deep lack
Or I can recognize my mistakes
And learn how to course correct

My child will feel
The residue of my projections
They are not hers to own
And I'm quick to acknowledge them

In the moment of fury
It's not easy to always see
But I know when I'm being reasonable
Or acting unconsciously

Owning my part
And recognizing my fears
Helps my child to understand
And not suppress them for years

Yet I know I'm not alone
When I dare to say
No matter my conscious efforts
She's bound to misinterpret them in some way

But I can't worry about the unknown
Or fear what may come to be
So long as I keep it real with my child
I know she will mirror that back to me

I will not always get it "right"
And will often get it "wrong"
Parenting isn't a destination
It's a journey of lessons that is life-long

Oh Dear Child

Oh dear child
So wise are thee
To know who you are
And defend your needs

To speak your mind
To honor your worth
To know in the moment
When your feelings are hurt

To create the inner space
So you can be still
To value your heart
With your fierce strong will

This wisdom you hold
Is remarkable to see
Even when I'm triggered beyond
By the way we are both being

When we are acting out
And lose sense of "control"
When our words and behavior
Leave imprints on our soul

It's not easy in the moment
To quickly see
The pain we are causing
Each other so deeply

Yet what I know
And what I feel
Is that no matter what
We keep real

We don't hold things in
Or pretend to be "perfect"
We are safe in expressing
And then work through it

I've given myself permission
To release any guilt and shame
When I show up unconscious
And have these types of days

Sometimes I need time
And my space
To recognize the lesson
I've been asked to embrace

May you feel my love
Even in our moments of despair
May you always know
How much I care

I know there are more
Teaching moments to come
For the union of our souls
Was a deliberate one

Oh dear child
So blessed am I
To walk this path with you
In this lifetime

Before My Eyes

Just like that
She's spreading her wings
She's soaring the winds
To discover new things

The fruits of our labor
Are beginning to take root
Where I was once taking the lead
She now chooses when to give me the boot

Her maturity is blossoming
Before my eyes
The things that once unsettled her
Now take me by complete surprise

Her ability to move forward
When something doesn't go her way
She finds other solutions
To satisfy her taste

Her season of growth
Is beautiful to see
Creating more space for freedom
And more space to be

Empowering her knowing
Encouraging her voice
Trusting her gut
So she can make a wise choice

She's coming into her own
And her confidence is clear
Her path is for the taking
Knowing there's nothing to fear

Your Child Knew Long Before

Long before your child
Was brought into your arms
They were making plans above
Before descending from the stars

They had watched you daily
Paying attention to your every move
Seeing how you handled your struggles
Deciding if you'd be able to handle theirs too

See they knew of their purpose
Before incarnating into this life form
So they choose wisely in advance
The parents in which to be born

But they weren't looking for perfection
As they understood the depths of "brokenness"
Was a part of every human being
In order to be here on earth and exist

So the child you have been given
While yours to guide and care for
Came directly to you with their own wisdom
For the sake of both your growth

And while you may not have realized
You, too, called them down from above
Because your souls were divinely connecting
Long before your journey here together had ever really begun

When our children feel safe in expressing their heart, voice,
feelings, thoughts, emotions and frustrations with us ...

knowing they will not be judged, shamed, belittled, condemned
or punished but rather heard, seen and validated

...we empower them to trust their own inner voice, to stand up
for themselves and to lead from their inherent place of truth.

Today's Children

The consciousness of today's children
Is unlike anything we've ever seen
Their vibrational energy is here
To dramatically change the way of things

They've descended with purpose
Each with their own unique gift
They've chosen their parents
Very knowingly to help them shift

From the old to the new
From the past to the now
Calling their parents to break the patterns
Empowering them to learn how

Today's children are more deeply attuned
To their inner world
More sensitive to their environment
Quick to speak their truth like never before

They will call someone out
Without an ounce of fear
They will challenge the status quo
If they don't like what they hear

They are warriors
They are might
They are authentic
They are bright

Our children of today
Are calling us to see
That through their spirits
How much wiser we can all be

She Is

She is beauty and peace
She is whole and sacred
She is love pulsating through my veins
She is wisdom in times of my pain

She is laughter and joy
She is thunder and rain
She is the unpredictable storm
She is my light and my strength

She is knowing and strong
She is gentle and kind
She is curious and daring
She is completely divine

She is restless and resilient
She is brave and courageous
She is pure and abundant
She is simply contagious

She is high energy and intuitive
She is outspoken and cautious
She is giving and thoughtful
She is vibrational and conscious

She is purpose
She is present
She is playful
She is protective

She is music and harmony
She is melody and song
She is artistic and creative
She is a force to reckon with all day long

She is a ray of sunshine
She is a spitfire on wheels
She is a negotiator with tenacity
She is a sensitive soul who deeply feels

She is a teacher of life
She is a guide to truth
She is an agent of change
She is an angel on earth

She has challenged me in ways
She knew I needed to grow
She's awakening parts of my being
Requiring me to surrender control

She's young
Though old in soul
She's been here lifetimes past
To change the status quo

She calls me mom
I call her love
She was the chosen spirit
Who chose me from above

Be a curious student of your child so you can remain open to their teachings.

How You Mirror Back to Me

Oh child
How you mirror back to me
The many ways I project
And for me to see

Where I fall short
In those moments of despair
When you scream or tantrum
Your behavior is begging me to hear

What your needs are
How you want to be heard
Where I'm pushing too hard
Why you feel misunderstood

My wisdom mind knows
When I have crossed the line
Reminding me to pause
So I can center and realign

And when I do
I can feel the shift
Both internally and externally
The tension begins to lift

We come back to together
And reconnect at our hearts
Sharing in a hug and kiss
To begin a fresh start

When Your Child Screams

When your child screams
It creates deep unease
Emotions runs high
Stress seduces the scene

You feel out of control
And so do they
But think of how your child is feeling inside
To make them act this way

You may instinctively react
In an unconscious way
Yet the greater challenge is to simply pause
And truly hear what your child is trying to say

I'm frustrated, I'm tired, I'm hungry, I'm sad
I'm helpless, I'm struggling, I'm scared, I'm mad
Don't beat me down any more than I feel
I'm just needing you to help me heal

You will more than likely experience
Feelings of lack or shame
But as long as you learn from it
There is no need to harbor any self-blame

Ask your child their perspective before projecting your views upon them.

I Get It

I get it
I truly do
Your child is screaming for what they want
And you feel a bit confused

Do I give in to them
To settle them down
Do I resist the fight
And stand my ground

The battle of the egos
Roaring loud and strong
Discerning in that moment
What is "right or wrong"

Asking *what is my fear*
That is getting in the way
Of hearing what my child's behavior
Is really trying to say

Attuning within
And getting really clear
Understanding all the moving parts
So you can begin to hear

The child before you
And your own inner child
Both that need nurturing
When their tempers run wild

Knowing when to pause
Knowing when to walk away
Knowing when to set a limit
This knowing doesn't happen in one day

It takes practice and time
Struggle and pain
It takes do-overs and reflection
If you want to co-create a new way

It takes patience and compassion
Love and understanding
It takes really knowing your child
If you've been called to help with their healing

More times than not
It's out of their control
They don't want to throw a tantrum
And feel internally miserable

The brain has a way
Of getting stuck in a rut
Especially with children
Whom are struggling with their gut

One change to their system
Can cause an internal mess
Even if that change you are making
Is ultimately for their best

No matter the reason
Or the cause
The struggle is real
The power is always in the pause

We cannot prevent our children from experiencing their pain.

This is a natural part of their life's unfolding.

What we can do is provide a safe space for them to feel and express their emotions, so they don't hold onto it unnecessarily.

To Be

When my child is *on*
I need to be *off*

When my child is *talking*
I need to be *silent*

When my child is *anxious*
I need to be *calm*

When my child is *questioning*
I need to *pause*

When my child is *active*
I need to be *still*

When my child is *angry*
I need to be *accepting*

When my child is *restless*
I need to be *restful*

When my child is *demanding*
I need to be *patient*

When my child is *happy*
I need to be *neutral*

When my child is *conflicted*
I need to be *connected*

When my child is *oppositional*
I need to be *approachable*

When my child is *disconnected*
I need to be *present*

When my child is *quiet*
I need to be *observant*

When my child is *reactive*
I need to be *responsive*

When my child is *needy*
I need to be *steady*

When my child is *scared*
I need to be *safe*

When my child is *avoidant*
I need to be *attuned*

When my child is *persistent*
I need to be *clear*

When my child is *sad*
I need to be *empathic*

When my child is *willing*
I need to be *ready*

When my child is *screaming*
I need to be *air*

When my child is *daring*
I need to be *cautious*

When my child is *sensitive*
I need to be *compassionate*

When my child is *wanting*
I need to be *guiding*

When my child is *playful*
I need to be *creative*

When my child is *seeking*
I need to be *curious*

When my child is *resistant*
I need to be *reflective*

When my child is *hitting*
I need to be *detached*

When my child is *loving*
I need to be *nurture*

When my child is *"out of control"*
I need to be *surrender*

When my child *is*
I need to *be*

My child is my greatest awakener.

The Light of The Moon

Goodnight sweet darling
It's time to sleep
Relax your mind, your heart and feet

Dream only of
Which will fill you up
Let go of any fears
That will cause you fuss

When you honor your body
And your soul
You will see how sleep
Is ever-so beautiful

And when you wake
The sun will too
For it's the light of the moon
That blissfully guided you through

The Depths of Motherhood

No one tells her
The depths she will go
Before bearing her child
She will need to bare her soul
To no one else
Other than herself

She had dreamed of motherhood
So innocently and pure
Little did she know
The pain she would endure
Not just from labor or the emotional rush
But from all inner feelings in which she'd lost touch

Of that little lost girl
Who had been waiting years inside
Begging to ask questions
And no longer willing to hide

Before you bear this new child
She pleads
Allow me this opportunity
To be heard and seen

I am you and you are me
I am here to set you free
So when your child comes from the heavens above
You are whole, abundant and ready to love

See I need you to understand
All of your inner 'broken' parts
So you are no longer disconnected
From your own sacred heart

It's time to awaken
All of your deepest fears
No longer can they stay suppressed
For any more years

Motherhood is more
Then raising of the child
It's a calling from *The Universe*
For you to fully rise

There will inevitably be bumps
And rough turns along the way
But your inner compass
Will never lead you astray

Your child chose you
Many years ago
And waited to descend into your arms
Until you were ready to let go
Only then could he or she show
Where you have yet to grow

So when your child is crying
Screaming and throwing a fit
Will you then know how
To handle and accept it

From a place of peace
Understanding and compassion
That you were once that same child
Needing attention

As much as you feel
You have to teach
Don't overextend
Or over preach

For the little soul
With whom you hold
Is here to teach you
More than you know

Motherhood is more
About mutual growth
Between child and mother
And the union of souls

*Your child comes to you with a request and you are
unsure whether you want to grant it or not –
don't react.*

Instead respond with "let me sit with it".

These five words hold so much power and presence.

Our Children Choose Us

Our children choose us
Long before they come through us
For they know from many lifetimes past
Who they wish to guide them on this life path

And through their intelligent zeal
They know what they need to heal
Here on earth in this life form
Which is why their spirit is called to be born

Their soul maps the way
Through infinite time and vast space
Aligning energetically their spirit to ours
With divine purpose that has always been written in the stars

Yet when our hearts finally collide
We both intuitively feel deep inside
The emergence of our respective karmic healing
That we have co-created together in this phyical life season

So if and when you question "why"
And find yourself on your knees with a hard cry
Understand that your spirit called your child to be your guide
To help you heal the wounds that have long resided inside

Paying Close Attention

Our children are paying close attention
To every move we make
From the way we do our hair
To the clothes we wear each day

From how we speak of our bodies
As we look into the mirror
Our children don't miss a beat
Capturing every word we share

From talking on the phone
To a friend or a business call
Our children learn the language of respect
First begins with how we treat ourselves

From the way we receive a compliment
To the way we offer one back
Our children embrace self-acceptance
Standing stronger in abundance than in lack

From how we handle conflict
Or how we may choose to avoid
Our children begin to form a belief
Of how to handle their emotions when they feel annoyed

From how we show up in the home
To the roles in which we play
Our children will come to believe
They must, too, do it the same way

From how we express our imperfections
To letting them know we are human
Our children will be self-compassionate
When they, too, experience frustrations

From how we take time to rest
To creating more time to breathe
Our children will embody this energy
Making their life more enjoyable and at ease

Parenting Is a Portal

Parenting is a gift
Wrapped up in disguise
Where your ego gets challenged
Through the essence of your child's eyes

It will help you see
And help you grow
It will impart lesson after lesson
It will break you open more than you know

Parenting is a portal
It will lead you deep within
It will beg of you questions
That you've been long holding in

When you feel so much love
For the soul who chose you
The sacred bond you made together
Will give you the strength to seek your truth

The ups and downs
The highs and lows
Parenting is a vessel
Where you are called to flow

With each wave
And each storm
The child you are to guide
Is here to help you transform

*It's been through my child's essence that I've had my
greatest breakdowns and breakthroughs.*

No Matter the Circumstances

We are love
We are strong
We are human
We will do "right and wrong"

No matter how frustrated we may get
No matter what we may say
No matter the circumstances
My love for you will never go away

I know you are trying your absolute best
I know how it can make you feel sometimes helpless
I know because I am trying too (and hope you can see)
On any given day, I am being the very best possible mommy

We both are emotionally tired
And feeling somewhat defeated
But together as a family
We are determined to see through it

We believe so much in the beautiful you
And want you to know
No matter what your brain is scaring into you
All things are ever-so possible

Please accept my apology
For the unkind things I've said
These are words that come from my own fear
And from my own unconscious head

You are an amazing light
Who fills up our lives
You are our angel forever
You are our whole life

Give Your Worries to Me

Give your worries to me sweet love
Know you're safe and protected from your angels above

Bedtime is when to let yourself unwind
Let go of your fears that take over your mind

For once you relax you will see
How your body will calm and simply be

And then you will drift off into your dreams
Building castles all while you sleep ever-so soundly

And when you awake the next day
The sun will greet you and shine the way

Give your worries to me sweet love
So your spirit can be free to experience the fun

As you create the space to nurture your own needs, your children will vibrate from that same energy.

True Warriors

Do you have a child
With different complexities
From high emotional struggles
To sensory processing and food sensitivities

Do you wonder how can this be
They are so young and innocent
What could be the cause or reason
For them to endure all of this

Well if you do
You're not alone
For there are thousands more
Who are braving the same storm

Being called upon this specific journey
Is one that requires a fierce heart
Becoming your own advocate
When you often feel alone in the dark

I have been one on this path
Who totally understands
What it means to rise to the call
And take matters in your own hands

There are so many variables
That lead to the root cause
Every child's body is different
Making the discovery often exhaustive

Our children are the true warriors
Who came here in this life form to heal
Even if we feel we're enduring the struggle
They are the ones whose struggle is real

Often feeling "different"
From what society considers "the norm"
When others around them can eat "anything"
While you're always bringing their food from home

And when they have a meltdown
It's not easy for them to settle and regulate
They can go from one extreme to another
All from a "wrong" food that they ate

But it's deeper than the surface
And far more than meets the eye
As the need beneath the behavior
Is the parent's endless search of "why"

It first starts with knowing
We are living in different times
From the soil in our ground
To our produce being full of pesticides

Toxins are everywhere
From household products and food
If our children lack proper gut health
It creates strong imbalances in their mood

Our genes, too, play a huge role
In the health of our child
If even one gene has a mutation
It can cause a lot of havoc inside

Then you add the stressors
In our everyday environment
That we consume at the deepest levels
Turning on and off our epigenetics

Our water travels through pipe systems
Contained with lead and copper
These heavy metals cause toxicity
Impacting how their bodies handle it

And when they get sick
Their bodies fight themselves
The medicines that are often given
Can do more "harm" than more help

There are so many factors at play
When ushering a child with "more needs"
It takes vigilance and commitment
To fully accept and receive

The honor in being their parent
And trusting what you know
How to guide them through their challenges
So they can heal, thrive and grow

Into their highest being
And share their innate gifts
Being the inspiration they are
And be in full self-acceptance

Always be proud of your child, not for what they do,
but merely for who they are.

What Is One Family's Struggle

I will try my best
To fully express
How as a mom I'm feeling inside

I'm not too proud
To speak my thoughts aloud
To show up boldly rather than hide

Maybe my share
Is meant for another to hear
To let them know they're not alone

As I sit on my couch
Half seated yet slouched
Typing this from my mobile phone

See there is a dis-ease
That can bring families to their knees
Should their child get sick with Strep

It's called PANDAS
And can suck the life out of 'ya
Leaving everyone feeling helpless

The symptoms overtake
In such a way
That your child can lose their mind

They become uncomfortable in their own skin
Obsessive thoughts and tics instantly begin
Setting your family's life "behind"

Sudden tantrums and rages
Irrational behaviors
Watching your child lose control

Helpless you stand
With the pressure and demand
To make sense of it all

There are so many ways
Strep can bring about this craze
One of them being in the gut

Prescribed antibiotics
Are sure to create deep havoc
And where everything gets f*d up

There are other things
Like one's immunity
That can make a child more susceptible

Where can bacteria invade
Parts of the brain
And attack the Basal Ganglia

But this dis-ease is little known
And has yet significantly grown
That traditional medicine denies

That's why it's so important
To be your own advocate
And really open your eyes

PANDAS will play out differently
In each kid you see
So don't try to compare

What is one family's struggle
May look different from another
Bottom line is deep despair

Next time your child may have Strep
Pay really close attention to it
And see if anything suddenly changes

One day they are doing fine
Living their life
Then next day having unexplainable rages

Yet my call to share
Doesn't end here
There is always a way light at the end of the tunnel

So seek out the help
In those moments you welp
For you and your child deserve the rest assured care

*It's when we stay clear within, detach from the
external perceptions or expectations of others,
attune to our child's true need underneath their behavior can we
then make a sound decision and lead from that place of knowing.*

She Just Wants to Be Seen

Her teenage heart
Full of laughter and dreams
Going about her life
So innocently it seemed

Then one day just like that
She's lost sight of it all
Somewhere in between the space of life
She began her fall

Darkness pervades her being
It strips the light from her heart
She threatens to take her life
She's depressed and emotionally "broken" in parts

She's lost trust and connection
To those she's closest too
She just needs someone to listen
And not tell her what to do

Helpless and confused
She loses her way
Making undesirable choices
Longing for someone to say

How can I help you
I'm here for you
I see you, you matter
I hear you too

I love you more than words can say
It pains me to know you are feeling this way
You don't have to say a word, just know you're enough, whole and worthy
I'm with you every step of the way

Though she's fighting her own thoughts
That are telling her deep lies
She's longing for guidance and safety
When you really see her cry

She feels alone and scared
And is suffering to stay alive
Her raging and abusive behaviors
Are her way to protect her heart on the inside

Connection is at the root
Which is the missing piece
Take a step back
To see what she truly needs

As she's pleading for help
And longing for inner peace
Simply hold the space
For her to be "as is" and release

Look within yourself
To see what this brings up in you
Your own fears, feelings and doubts
Of the helplessness of not knowing what to do

She needs you more
Than she's leading to you believe
Next time she pushes you away
Dig deep to find compassion and empathy

If she reaches for your hand
Yet resists at the same time
She's testing the waters to see
If you will hold steady the line

Once you create the space within your own being
To not react and see her in her purest essence
She will slowly open up
And you will organically create a deeper connection and presence

You Are Human

Did you hear your child say *mom*
A thousand times or so it seemed
To the point your ears went numb
And you wanted to just scream

Did you hold your patience well
Then all of a sudden you cracked
When you repeat yourself over and again
And got triggered just like that

Did you stay conscious to your words
In some moments of your day
But when things got stressed
You went completely the other way

Did you go with the flow
Staying as present as can be
When your child was having imaginary play
You were anticipating when to clean

Did you remind yourself you're human
When the going gets tough
Holding yourself with love and compassion
When the day-to-day can be too much

Did you see all that you accomplished
And what it took to show up
Through the "good, bad and indifferent"
Give yourself some love

*Follow the flow of your
child's essence.*

Let their spirit lead the way.

*For it will guide and align with
The Universe's plan for their being to serve both themselves and others.*

Warrior Moms

Warrior moms show up ready
Even when they're half undone
They will put aside their own needs
More often than not to support their beloved ones

Warrior moms jump into the fire
No matter how hot it burns
They will do whatever it takes
To help their children thrive at every possible turn

Warrior moms are on call
They keep on alert at all times
Never knowing when they are needed
They'll drop everything on a dime

Warrior moms are strong-hearted
They can conquer the unimaginable
Even when they feel helpless
They are committed and dependable

Warrior moms take the lead
From morning until night
They plan, create and execute
Having great vision and foresight

Warrior moms are defenders
They will put on their armor to protect
Whatever circumstances arise
They are their children's greatest advocate

Warrior moms are authentic
They don't pretend they can do it all
In their moments of great despair
They give themselves permission to just ball

Warrior moms are not just women
They, too, are warrior dads
Who assume the main role of caretaker
And support their young lads

Her Light

When I became a first-time momma
To the most amazing baby girl
What I could not have known then
Is how her light would change my world

She holds limitless power
Her heart is full of love
How blessed am I that she
Requested me from above

She descended on her own time
For her soul knew the way
The path we were called to embark
Would require vigilance and undeniable strength

I don't think I could have known
All that I was going to receive
The blessings and the trials
The day that I had conceived

Her warrior spirit is fierce
Her trust in life is divine
There isn't a day that passes
That she doesn't simply blow my mind

Has every moment been blissful
Without struggle or pain
It's been in these precise experiences
That I've undoubtedly evolved and changed

Because of you my dear
I'm a better version of me
You've rocked my world beyond measure
And I'm grateful to you for eternity

Each day we walk this journey
Together side by side
May you always feel my love
Deep deep down inside

I love how authentic we are
How safe we feel to express
I love that you know intuitively
We are always "doing" our best

And though you are
Beyond your years
May all your dreams come true
Don't let them be held back by your fears

The world is your oyster
Go take it by storm
There isn't a doubt in my mind
Your light is here to help others transform

The first language our children learn is not through our actual words.

It is through the vibration of our energy that
speaks the language of love or fear.

Empowering Our Children

Empowering our children to use their voice
Is one of the greatest powers they'll know
Hearing the resonance of their own truth
Becomes their inner compass for self-growth

It will lead them in the direction
To ask questions before they agree
Even if it causes the other
A bit of discomfort and uncertainty

Teaching them to understand
Their voice is sacred and strong
Not to be disrespectful of it
Or do it any "wrong"

Instead to regard its innate power
Its purpose and its place
Always upholding the vibrations
Of oneness love and soulful grace

As they exercise their voice
In order to stand up for what feels right
May we walk alongside them in courage
In those moments they feel the inner fight

Our children today are unlike
Any generations past
They've been called from a higher consciousness
To awaken us and break through "the glass"

Of the old ways of staying quiet
Where voices were not heard
Do as you were told
Respect your elder

We cannot evolve as a nation
As a world, as a whole
If we ourselves don't disrupt the patterns
That keep us silenced and small

Let's take more time to listen
To hear what our children have to say
Let's stay in full awareness
And begin to pave the way

So they feel more safe to speak up
And worthy and seen
Feel valued in their heart
And infinitely accepted in their divine being

Allow Me to Guide You

Come child
Take my hand
Allow me to guide you
The best I can

Keep your eyes wide open
Pay attention to all you see
Stay curious along the way
Question everything

If I move too fast or rush you
Please speak up and say so
Don't be afraid to tell me
What your heart already knows

The journey we're on together
Will challenge and grow us strong
There will be mistakes we both make
But it doesn't mean we are "wrong"

I will always ensure your safety
This is a guarantee
Even in those moments
You are ready to set your wings free

The foundation in which I set
Is built with everlasting love
No matter where your own path takes you
You are my earth angel sent from above

I thank you for choosing me
And trusting me to care for you
May our hands stay forever connected
While we walk this lifetime living our truth

Find the alchemy in those big emotional moments with your child.

*For they are leading you to go deeper to discover
the treasure to your self-growth.*

Vulnerability and Empowerment

*Just as a rose opens through the ray of sunlight, so does
your soul's calling through its own inner light.*

Permission to Feel

Allow yourself *permission to feel*
Whatever is needing to come up
Let your heart begin to heal
Nurture those wounded parts with love

Do not question or condemn it
For it has already been much suppressed
Let your inner child know for once
In this moment you will no longer regress

Bring clarity to your voice
Adjust the tone in your ears
Expand your arms wide open
So you can release all of your fears

Listen for the unspoken
Hear what is not being said
Attune deep within your soul
Be still and be led

By your inner knowing and truth
By the guidance of your light
Give yourself the permission
To surrender to your inner fight

Breathe in freedom from the air
Dance merrily about
Exhale any restrictive energies
That may be causing you self-doubt

Permission to be as you are
Without any external validation
Is the only permission you need
To find your beautiful salvation

189

Self-Love

For some you'll be too much
For others not enough
It's not yours to own
Stay focused on self-love

What another sees in you
Something they like or not
Is a reflection of themselves
Guiding them to wake up

See the energy we exchange
Holds more power than we know
It can trigger and hold us back
Or merely propel us all to grow

An example is with my child
How contagious we both can be
The slightest upset can happen
When we are out of synergy

Or on the opposite end
We can be joyful and at play
Those are the moments
When we've been in alignment that day

I am constantly reminded
How our energy is infused
This is how we all interact
Start noticing so you're not confused

It may be someone you know
Or someone you just meet
Our auras are always projecting
Filling in gaps where there is "need"

So when you feel a bit of lack
And start to think it's you
Consider your surroundings
For it may have everything to do

With how the other is attracted
To your particular energy
It can complement yours
Or leave you feeling empty

For some you'll be too much
For others not enough
It's not yours to own
Stay focused on self-love

Meeting Your True Self

The moment you meet
Your true self
You will feel at home
Like nowhere else

An instant knowing
Will wash over your heart
You will embrace your truth
Ready and willing to embark

Upon the path
You were always destined to be
One with your true self
Fully and authentically

An immediate self-acceptance
Of who you know you are
Will guide you deeper
Letting go of all the false parts

It's like reconnecting
With a long-lost friend
Not missing a beat
Aligning to your natural harmony again

You will gain a sense of peace
An unspoken resonance inside
When you meet your true self
Is the moment you will truly come alive

The Place in Which You Are

There is no place to get to
There is no place to leave behind
The place in which you are
Is exactly where you are to align

Not a moment sooner
Are you to be
This moment you are in
Is an opportunity to see

That the more you force your way
The greater resistance you will meet
This is when you surrender
So you can discover your own unique beat

When you pay attention to the notes
That only your soul instrument is to play
You can tune out the other noises
That want to get in your way

Who you are is unique
And impacts the rest
It's a co-creation of all things
That amplifies our collective best

There is abundance in life
Even in the depths of lack
The cause and effect of it all
Is where *The Universe* always has your back

Don't Dim Your Light

Don't dim your light,
Don't lower your voice
Don't give up the "fight"
Because you always have a choice

A choice in how you receive
A choice in what you give
In this lifetime be the example
In how you choose to live

When doubt dances in your thoughts
And fear races through your mind
That is an invitation to stop, pause and breathe
To look forward and no longer look behind

What has past is in the past
The present is now what is here
Go inward more closely
To find what is really there

Ask yourself
What am I feeling deep within my core
Is this a way for me to pay attention to
What is there and no longer ignore

Often we silence the authentic noise in our heads
Through a story we create to make us feel better instead

Only when we fully awaken and allow ourselves to just be
Will we really know how to shine our essence-filled
light for all others to see

Tears are not a sign of weakness.

They are a connection to one's
self-expression of inner truth.

Do You Dare

Do you dare to speak up
Even when you feel the fear
Do you dare to trust your heart

Do you dare to say no
Even when you feel the urge
Do you dare to use your voice

Do you dare to choose differently
Even when you feel scared
Do you dare to stand in your truth

Do you dare to walk away
Even when you feel afraid
Do you dare to take the higher road

Do you dare to cry your eyes
Even when you feel the ego rise
Do you dare to release your pain

Do you dare to start anew
Even when you feel content
Do you dare to seek something greater

Do you dare to ask for help
Even when you feel lonely
Do you dare to reach out your hand

Do you dare to say *it's hard*
Even when you feel the struggle
Do you dare to be vulnerable

Do you dare to shut your mouth
Even when you feel the need to talk
Do you dare to be silent

Do you dare to be still
Even when you feel the need to do
Do you dare to let go and let be

Do you dare to take ownership
Even when you feel no fault
Do you dare to see the role you play

Do you dare to trust the now
Even when you feel impatient
Do you dare to surrender and trust

Every Experience

Every experience is an opportunity to grow
To connect within to what you innately know
To awaken your heart and open your mind
To access your strength through the Divine

Every experience is an opportunity to feel
To decipher what is fiction and what is real
To discover the depths of your soul
To remind yourself that you are inherently whole

Every experience is an opportunity to see
To trust what is here is meant to be
To surrender the want and need "to know"
To allow the discomfort while being in flow

Every experience is an opportunity to hear
To attune to the whispers in your ear
To listen to the calling from above
To rise in your truth through your love

She Wonders

Amidst her day
In between laundry and cooking
She wonders
She dreams
She asks
Am I enough

When everyone's asleep
In between paying bills and preparing lunches
She wonders
She dreams
She thinks
Do I matter

While taking a quick break
In between sipping tea and calling a friend
She wonders
She dreams
She feels
What is my purpose

Alone in her bed
In between her tears and self-reflection

She wonders
She dreams
She trusts
She believes
She lets go
She knows

She matters
She's enough
She's divinely on purpose

Only when we can begin to heal our inner world can
we begin to see an outer world that is healed.

True Strength

Strength is often mis-measured by how we show up externally
Putting on our "game face" and keeping it all
together but falling apart internally

Saying *I'm doing fine* when asked about our day
Not wanting to appear weak in any kind of way

True strength is being able to cry and
not care what others think
Asking for help so you don't reach for that drink

Not hiding and facing your pain
Getting most real with yourself looking for nothing to gain

Saying *I'm not doing well* when someone asks how you are
Simply breaking down and allowing yourself to just fall apart

Strength looks messy and yet so beautiful
Strength deepens one's connection to their own divine soul

Strength tells a story of truth that is undisguised
Strength reveals itself holding back no lies

Strength is powerful though not just in physical form
Strength is often quiet while sitting through the storm

Strength cleanses the body as the tears fall upon the face
Strength is gentle, non-judgmental and offers grace

Strength is knowing when to surrender and trust
Strength is the innate wisdom within each and every one of us

Her Wings

Her wings were made to fly
Through the vast and infinite sky
Through the darkness and the light
Her wings carry her day and night

Her wings are a place of rest
When she's given her absolute best
When she's taken all she can
Her wings become her trusted friend

Her wings take her to new heights
To challenge her strength inside
To open and expand her heart
Her wings keep her ready to start

Her wings often feel defeated
They are overworked and feel cheated
They are stretched far and wide
Her wings themselves need to cry

Her wings are searching and seeking
For growth in every season
For wisdom in every storm
Her wings keep her safe and warm

Her wings are gentle yet strong
Where no turn she takes is "wrong"
Where no place she lands is "right"
Her wings are her guiding light

Her wings change color and form
When she takes the path to conform
When she shields the pain she feels
Her wings are a safe place to heal

Her wings are heaven on earth
Protecting others from hurt
Protecting the sacred environment
Her wings are salvation and confinement

Her wings nourish the mouths of babes
Around the clock each day
Around the chaos of life
Her wings protect souls in strife

Her wings were chosen for her
No one else was called to serve
In the way she was asked to rise
And spread her wings across the sky

You Matter

Your purpose is divine and purposeful
Full of life and breath
Full of hope and possibility

It is designed only for you
To share with the world

Your essence is destined for greatness
Everything you are and all you need
Is already seeded within your soul

With the fibers of your spirit
Through your brilliance and bravery
Through your story and struggles
You were called here to serve humanity
With your purpose

Through your pain
Through your inner power
However big or small
Your purpose matters
You matter
Don't let anyone tell you otherwise

When you fully accept yourself
Every ounce of who you are
When you embrace your imperfections
Allow grace to sit by your side

Can you begin to hear the whispers in your heart
Without judgment or guilt
Without shame
Without fear or failure

Only with love and compassion
With honor and trust
Have faith and believe

You are here to share your difference

Ignite Your Light

What is blocking you from seeing
Your own truth and light
Why do you feel "lesser than"
Yet believing others are more bright

Where did this dialogue start
That you've become numb to it for so long
Whose voice do you hear in your head
That has lead you to believe you are "wrong"

No one has the answers
Better than you do within
So stop looking everywhere else
And start asking *how do I begin*

To see my purpose
To feel my heart
To speak my truth
To be my own North Star

To live my passion
To embrace my dreams
To know my worth
To dare life to the extreme

To nurture my soul
To hold my own hand
To love my being
To know my power where I stand

What is blocking you from seeing
Your own truth and your own light
The world needs your gifts
To guide them through their own fight

Rise tall
Reach far
Look deep within
To ignite your heart

I Am

I am a student of life
A curious soul
I am fascinated by each person
I come to know

I can feel rather quickly
The energy of the other
I am able to discern
When I should inquire or not bother

I am often unconventional
In my style and way
Staying true to my being
Not concerned with what the others say

I show up in my truth
I speak from my heart
I realize not everyone I meet
Will appreciate this human art

I attune within
To take a check on me
I course correct my energy
When I find I am out of sync

I am reflective and nostalgic
I am an old soul
I can see as I get older
I've been here many lifetimes before

I enjoy my own company
I don't need much to be entertained
Silence and quietude I find
Are the places most I play

I love to write poetry
As an expression of my healing
In my words I find peacefulness
And deep meaning

I am not my role as mother
I am not my role as wife
I am a spiritual being experiencing
This human form of life

I am grateful for each moment
Albeit "good or bad"
For I know *The Universe*
Always has my back

When you release the need "to need", you make space within your being to be freed.

Trust and Patience

Never let go of a dream.

It will show up when it is ready to be born.

In its own time.

Trust

When you feel a tug in your heart
Or a pit in your gut
These are often intuitive signs
To get you out of your rut

It's your body conveying
And letting you know
Your patterns need disrupting
So you can explore deeper growth

Though you may question
And choose not to "comply"
For fear of the unknown
And trusting your "why"

It's okay to feel scared
And have your doubts
Anytime we go through changes
A lot of uncertainty comes about

Because we've been conditioned
To follow a set way
Trusting there is more for us
Then how we're living today

See every one of us
Made a contract with our soul
That's why we incarnated
Into this physical form

And when we realize
The value of this gift
We will not question the signs
And instead proceed with grit

We will serve the call
And trust what we cannot see
Allowing our heart to speak to us
So we can live this life as we were meant to be

It's Not Your Time

So often you wish
For something to be
Praying and wishing
You are unable to see

That the space between the want
And the true need
Is the space where time is planted
So *The Universe* can nourish the seeds

That period of gestation
Can be ever so magical
A lot can transpire
To help you strengthen and grow

When you hear another say
It's not your time
May you understand the meaning
As one to be perfectly divine

This is not always something
That you may accept
It's the resistance of your mind
Impatiently waiting to get

Yet once the picture gets more clear
Will you then be able to see
That time was always on your side
From the very beginning

Dear Patience

We have traversed this life together for over forty
decades and I want you to know ...

You have kept me safeguarded and out of harm's way

You have helped steer me on the right course
when I lost focus to see clearly

You've allowed me the opportunity to pause and think through
some of the biggest life decisions I've had to make

You've given me the space to breathe when I was on the verge of tears

You have reminded me of my inner power in those
moments when I lost faith in myself

You have been gentle with giving me the necessary
time when I was being demanding

You have kept me grounded when I was seeking control

You have aligned the stars as they were intended to
connect me to my destiny as it was meant

You have trusted the process and shown me through
you that *The Universe* is guiding the way

You have allowed me to fall so I could learn
the true depths of your purpose

You have invested the energy to keep up with my highs and lows

You have held the boundary even when I've pushed against you

You have taught me how to surrender while keeping
my finger on the pulse of my calling

You have allowed me to see that all before me
is truly for my growth and evolution

You have empowered me to take ownership of my
behaviors when I'm feeling lack-minded

You have proven to me that everything happens in its own time

You have kept me from speaking unwanted words

You have been the window to my inner wisdom

You have challenged me beyond measure knowing the
distance I need to go to feel the pain of the process

You have given me grace when I could have been in guilt

You have tested me powerfully in ways I never
thought I'd be able to handle a situation

You have rewarded me with a life that I'm
grateful to live fully and learn fiercely

You have been constant even when I've been inconsistent with you

Patience you are
Like the North Star
Whose light shines bright
For all to see

While there are days
I lose sight
Of your guiding light
I am reminded to simply be

Be in touch with your true power
In those waking hours
Where I simply want "to know"

Patience you are
Never a distance too far
To keep me safe and in your flow

As I Surrender

As I surrender
I can begin to taste
The freedom of my breath

I can feel the weight
In its release
That no longer feels like death

I am able to embody
The sensations within
Connecting more to my body, mind and soul

I am removing the bars
That I once lived behind
Allowing my truth to be exposed

I am witnessing layers
Being peeled and shed
That have taken up space for too long

As I surrender
I remain curious and open
To the continued growth to come

What We Cannot See

You aren't given more than you can handle
Though the weight may be more than you can bear
What doesn't kill you makes you stronger
These are the phrases we will so often hear

When we've reached a point of frustration
Or are ready to drop to our knees
Somehow the strength lying deep within us
Carries us beyond our own belief

When we are walking through the fire
Feeling the burning sensations of our pain
We seldom can see the purpose
Or think we have anything to gain

For at the moment we are questioning
And cursing and screaming out loud
It is in that very moment
We should be silent and simply allow

Trust what we cannot see
See what we cannot know
Know what we cannot hear
Hear what will make us grow

Life has its unique ways
Of teaching us lessons through love
Even if we don't understand it in that moment
The Universe IS always one within us

Though you may not see your wings,
take flight because you are meant to fly.

Everything Always Works Out

There was a time
Not that long ago
When I felt restless and unsettled
Not knowing where to go

I questioned my purpose
And felt conflicted in my heart
Desiring more than I had
Not sure where to start

It seemed everyone else
Was following their dreams
Going about life happily
From what it seemed

What was wrong with me
I would think and say
That I can't figure out
The path of life I wanted to take

It was only when
I stopped pushing so hard
Was I able to hear
The calling within my own heart

You are right where you are
As you are meant to be
For the journey you're traversing
Will reveal its deepest meaning

You must stay patient
And trust The Universe's plan
While it may not make any sense now
You will soon come to understand

And in between this knowing
And space and time
My daughter's spirit found me
Her presence changed my life

I could never have known
All she would awaken in me
Parts of my soul
That brought me to my knees

That was only
Eight short years ago
To think of how far we've come
And have yet to grow

I no longer question
Or harbor any doubt
Trusting my journey is divine "as is"
Believing everything always works out

One with The Water

I can feel the ocean of waves you are facing and that are consuming you

Yet in this vast space you are suffocating

The high tides crashing against your heart
All the while you are needing to feel safe within

As you swim ashore treading water
Breathing heavily to stay above
Needing a life jacket to keep you from drowning

And as you navigate the rough waters
You must first serve and soothe your inner child's needs

So tap into your heart space and find the love
language to soothe your inner child
Letting them know they are safe

In this knowing and surrender
You will feel carried and guided by the water
Trusting the direction of each wave's flow

Let the waters reflect your own inner compass
Stay in your truth
Guide from your essence

You will arrive at the shore with great peace
and strength more than you started with

When life gives you a blank canvas paint
it with passion.

Purpose in All That Unfolds

Everything happens for a reason
There is purpose in all that unfolds
From the darkest of pain and sorrow
Comes a blessing in disguise to hold

It's in how we choose to receive
The gift in our grief
That will determine our own ability
To turn it into alchemy

This doesn't diminish the emotions
Which we must inevitably go through
For it's in the process of those feelings
That strengthens our character too

Just as the seed must be planted
In order for it to grow
So must our trust in *The Universe*
Be deeply rooted in our soul

Everything happens for a reason
There is possibility in all we allow
From the moment we choose abundance
Comes the answers in the now

225

Meant to Be

Did your day turn out as you expected
Was it better or was it worse
Did you traverse the path of discomfort
Or heed the guidance from *The Universe*

Did you find yourself frustrated
Projecting your anxieties onto your child
Did you take a pause in that given moment
Or stay unconscious and let your mind run wild

Did you see your story play out
Were your thoughts hijacking your mind
Did you own your part in the day
Or blame others for being unkind

Did you hold self-compassion
Nurture your sacred heart
Did you give yourself permission
Or self-sabotage and just fall apart

Did you try best
In light of your day
Did you hold gratitude
Or wish it played out another way

Did you stop to smell the roses
Capture nature and its divine grace
Did you stop to look in the mirror
And see the reflection of its beauty in your own face

May you enter each day with open arms
May you receive the blessings in disguise
May you connect not only deeper within
But more deeply into the other's eyes

May you see you are not alone
May you feel heard and seen
May you trust and know the path you walk
Is meant for your highest being

Trusted My Knowing

I trusted my knowing
And took a leap of faith
When I picked up and left my comfort zone
Moving away for the first time to another state

I trusted my knowing
And said *I do*
After thirty-five years of being single
Wondering when I would get married and to whom

I trusted my knowing
And it proved to be divine
When I stopped controlling the process
Allowing my child to be born on her time

I trusted my knowing
And still landed on my feet
When I quit my high paying job
Letting go of my fears of the money

I trusted my knowing
And my child is thriving more
When I began seeing her signs of struggle
Believing in the power of a cure

I trusted my knowing
And began writing as a way to heal
When I felt frustrated and confused
Giving my heart the inner space to truly feel

I trusted my knowing
And still find moments of doubt
After *The Universe* has shown me otherwise
Teaching me I still have a long way to go for now

You may not yet see what it is the future holds for you but rest knowing the light within you is illuminating the way.

Silence and Reflection

Rain is to nature what a good cry is to the soul.

An act of self-love.

Embodying its divine energy.

Nourishing its true spirit.

Accepting its own beauty.

Sit with Your Feelings

Sit with your feelings
Allow them to stir
There will be moments of clarity
And others a blur

Listen to your heart
Be gentle with your soul
There will be times you know "for sure"
And moments you won't

Cry out your tears
Mourn the depths of any loss
There will be glimpses of hope
And others where you feel completely lost

Give yourself permission
Surrender to the unknown
There will be times you are scared shitless
And others where you take life by storm

Fully accept your humanness
Embrace your spirit as one
There will be parts of yourself that you rediscover
And others that feel long gone

Sit with your feelings
Allow them to flow
In those moments of their movement
Let go and just unfold

Everyone is Searching

Are you paying attention
Are you looking around
Do you see the patterns and themes
That are breaking people down

Everyone is searching
High and low
Seeking to find "answers"
Everywhere they go

Unhappy with who they are
Scrolling anxiously on their phone
Comparing themselves to others
That they don't even know

Living half empty
Numbing their problems and fears
Disconnected from their truth
That perhaps stemmed from their childhood years

No fault of their own
They had to survive
Their parents' unconsciousness
And still finding a way to thrive

My heart truly bleeds
For those I hear and see
How many people are living
In complete and utter misery

Though it's not my story
I can genuinely feel
How so many people
Struggle to keep it real

Pain is subjective
And can never be compared
However deep one's void
Requires continuous love and care

It all comes down to knowing
Who we truly are
So we can be liberated
From taking on others' scars

"Easier said than done"
Might be one's easy excuse
When they would rather deny
Then discovering their deepest truth

But at the end of the day
We all have a choice
To stay stuck where we are
Or find our inner voice

To stand up for ourselves
To reclaim our power
To get rid of what no longer
Serves our highest honor

So long as we are breathing
And we are becoming aware
The path we endeavor
Is one to be dared

So stop the patterns
That are destructive to you
Begin waking up
However you have to

Start with silence
So you can go within
Listen for the answers
It's one place to begin

Enter the Here and Now

Enter the here
And now
Let go of the pressure
And just allow

Trust your heart
And be in flow
Release expectations
For your instincts just know

Don't overthink
Of the way it's to be
The moment you're in
Will help you see

That when you show up
As you are
The Universe becomes
Your guiding star

Dear Universe

You are one with me as I am one with you
You are the invisible who knows my truth

You pull me in closer to you when I go astray
You whisper to my soul *everything is going to be okay*

You lead me to the path that I may have otherwise missed
You ask me to take my hands off the wheel
reminding me that *you got this*

You can see when I'm impatient and desiring control
You tug at my gut saying *you don't need to know*

You are love
You are air
You are breath
You are light

You are love
You are hope
You are trust
You wise

You are truth
You are divine
You are heart
You are soul

You are consciousness
You are knowing
You are powerful
You are purposeful

You are energy
You are guiding
You are connectedness
You are evolution

You are freedom
You are peace
You are essence
You are expansive

You are presence
You are compassionate
You are open
You are accepting

You are authentic
You are pure
You are laughter
You are healing

You are awareness
You are non-judgmental
You are forgiving
You are silence

You are nature
You are intelligent
You are patient
You are kind

You are generous
You are limitless
You are soulful
You are source

If I haven't said it aloud today or if I should forget again
tomorrow, *I thank you for being the foundation to my own being*

Thank you for holding me up when I need to fall
For helping me to tap deep within and learn to stand tall

Thank you for being patient with me when my mind goes awry
For gently nudging me to give it another try

Thank you for allowing me the grace when I struggle to let go
For empowering me within to surrender and be in the flow

Thank you for trusting in me when I seem to lose sight
For keeping your hand on my heart to ignite my inner light

Thank you for giving me the power to choose
Never judging me when I "should" happen to lose

Thank you for giving me the space to be free
Encouraging me to step more into my creativity

Because of you
I am me
We are one together
For eternity

Feel the Rain

Feel the rain
But don't let it drench your dreams

Feel the wind
But don't let it sweep you off your feet

Feel the ground
But don't let it keep you standing still

Feel the breath
But don't let it suffocate your spirit

Feel the pain
But don't let it hold you back

Feel the cold
But don't let it freeze your heart

Feel the heat
But don't let it fester up the anger

Feel the solitude
But don't let it keep you separate

Feel the tears
But don't let it keep you scared

Feel the confusion
But don't let it get you lost

Feel the happiness
But don't let it consume you

Feel the sadness
But don't let it bring you down

Feel the loneliness
But don't let it keep you alone

Feel the feelings
Just as they are
Go within and allow them to surface
Without creating judgment or emotional scars

Feel the feelings
And hold the space
Watch them like mere tidal waves
With presence and grace

Feel the feelings
Without reaction or resistance
Accept them in their fullness
A divine part of your presence

Ground

We are never in one place too long
To feel our feet holding us up
To feel our legs standing strong

We are here but we are nowhere
Doing yet seeking
Thinking yet dreaming
Moving yet pausing

We are walking through life half awake
To see what we want
To want what we can't see
To connect to our divinity

We are spinning our wheels and going too fast
To keep up with the world
To not miss a beat
To find meaning on our path

It's when we get still
Only then can we drown out the sounds
Of all that we think is
Instead connecting our being to the ground

*The only contract that truly matters is
the one with your soul.*

All the rest are man-made.

The Breath

It beholds the beauty
That gives us life
The breath is steady and is wise

It brings us closer
To our heart
The breath is a neutralizer when we fall apart

It gives without asking
And allows us to be
The breath is a precious commodity

It is sometimes ignored
When we rush through the day
The breath will never lead us astray

It is a loving companion
That supports our needs
The breath is a gift to cherish indeed

Heart Wisdom

Our heart is a treasure box
Where we hold sacred the jewels to our soul
Where we hold the key to either protect or proclaim its riches
Where we access the value of its inherent worthiness

Our heart is a vessel
Where we carry the nutrients of love
Where we hold the remnants of pain
Where we transport the breath of life

Our heart is a safety net
Where we risk the leap
Where we surrender the grip
Where we walk freely

Our heart is a memoir
Where we speak our authentic voice
Where we write our inner truth
Where we read our depths of wisdom

Our heart is a canvas
Where we paint our vision
Where we portray our inner landscape
Where we illustrate our infinite beauty

Our heart is a blanket
Where we comfort the wounded memories
Where we rest the mind with peace
Where we warm the inner child with ease

Family Tree

Its roots are the foundation
For which its fruits are bore
It weathers the storms
To provide

Its seeds are the nourishment
For which its fruits can grow
It feeds the hands
To thrive

Its branches are the landing
For which its leaves can soar
It seeks no shelter
To grow

Its leaves are the playground
For which its freedom is expressed
It blows with the wind
To find

The family tree is built to withstand
Hold steady and be strong
Endure the unforeseen wreckage
And find its way to carry on

With grace and ease
With determination and strength
With trust and peace
With love and faith

The family tree is grounded
Yet able to bend
It protects from harm
And is prepared to mend

The family tree is one
With each of its parts
It cycles its life
Connects at the heart

Its breath is found
In the spaces between
The roots and branches
The fruits and leaves

The family tree has seasons
It changes colors in the light
While it also blocks the darkness
Its essence always shines bright

The family tree is community
It gathers amongst other trees
It shares a commonality
In the beauty of peace

When the roots weaken
And begin to die
The heavens above
Shower down their powerful cry

It cleanses the air
It dampens the grounds
It nurtures new roots
And breeds a new round

The family tree is you
It is me
It is us
It fully surrenders to the not knowing
With complete and utter trust

The Meaning of Home

Home means something different
For each and everyone
Conventional in form
Yet non-traditional for some

Home is where the heart is
No matter the place
It's the feeling one carries inside them
That creates warmth within that space

Home is a vibration
That doesn't require walls
Its foundation is built on love and energy
Where the doors are open to all

Home is within you
Its breath resides in your heart
The strength of its wind carries you
When any pieces come apart

Home means something different
For each and everyone
No matter the way you see it
May it be filled with peace and love

It is only through our mistakes that we grow.

So, go easy on yourself through your continued unfolding as a human being.

Accept responsibility for any missteps you make and
keep looking for the signs to guide you
back on your path.

Most importantly, listen deeply to your
inner voice as it will never steer you wrong.

A Guide

A guide leads you to the mountain
And inspires you to climb
They empower you to reach higher
One step at a time

A guide echoes the whispers
That are already in your heart
They help you to hear the truth
Providing the motivation for you to start

A guide firmly pushes
But gently lets go
Giving you just enough space
To figure it out so you can grow

A guide calls it as it is
Even if it means you will be upset
They are not worried if you don't like them
As their purpose is for you to have no regrets

A guide helps you to set boundaries
In a way for you to see
What is yours alone to own
And what is yours to release

A guide walks alongside you on your path
Offering many different options you can take
They will encourage your every effort
And support you when you make a mistake

A guide shares its wisdom
As a reflection of your own soul
Helping you to access your power
While staying aligned to life's flow

Sometimes

It takes losing hope to find faith

It takes breaking down to build back up

It takes getting lost to be found

It takes being silent to hear the noise

It takes experiencing the pain to feel the purpose

It takes a deep breath to connect to the now

It takes getting frustrated to lean into the freedom

It takes walking through darkness to arrive at the light

It takes falling down to stand back high

It takes witnessing the lies to see the truth

It takes going through the problem to reach the solution

It takes asking the questions to listen for the answers

It takes working through the complexities to deconstruct the simplicity

It takes crying unabashedly to heal the wound

It takes getting raw to get real

Silver Lining

It is often so hard to see
What the ultimate purpose may be
When we are deep in our pain
It's hard to see the silver lining in the rain

The clouds mask our view
Not knowing how we will get through
How this moment will pass
Or how long these feelings will last

It can feel like we are alone
No one around for us to hold
Needing to release a deep cry
Questioning aloud "how come and why"

This process can be so deep
Often bringing us to our knees
And learn to truly let go
So we can experience greater self-growth

It is often so hard to see
What the ultimate purpose may be
But when we allow the storm to pass
That is when the silver lining will cast

Stream of Consciousness

By the end of the night I'm drained
Does any other parent feel the same

I can't imagine I'm alone
Whether you go to an office
Or work from home

It's hard to balance it all
Being a parent you are always on call

Though our kids are asking nothing more
Than to simply support their needs
In between the daily chores
We show up often half present, exhausted and on bended knees

It's a different world in which we parent
From even twenty years ago
Technology has changed the game
It is a balance of surrender and control

Many of us are parenting
At a later stage in life
And the children called to guide us
Are more strong-willed than ever and full of gusto and might

So naive were we to believe
That parenting would be a breeze
We got the exact child we needed
To help us grow and wake us from our fantasy

For me parenting has broken me open
And often broken me down
I am still learning daily
How to live in the present moment, in the now

I chose to quit my career
When my daughter turned one
While it has been the best decision I have made
It is not a sacrifice for everyone

I had expectations and visions
Of the way it was "supposed" to be
Thinking when she goes to school full-time
I would be getting back to me

And on those more challenging days
I often find I pray
I ask *The Universe*
How much more of this can I truly take

My intellect reasons
My heart holds the space
My wisdom rises
As I see the lessons I am being asked to embrace

What I did not know at the time
Was that my agenda did not align
With what *The Universe* had in its own mind
As it whispers in my ear

The child who chose you
Chose you well
You are not behind on your plan
For where you are in this moment
Is exactly where you're meant to stand

Helping to heal your child
As you heal yourself
This is your purpose
My plan for you
And from this will come all else

—

Trust is golden
Patience is key
When I am feeling scattered and lost
I find silence to simply be

With my thoughts
With my feelings
With my doubts
With my fears
I then cleanse my soul
By releasing my tears

There is no shame in it
Sometimes it is all you need
To recalibrate your mind
To reconnect to inner peace

Go deep within to discover your own treasure.

Reflections of The Day

There is silence in the air
Night fall graces the sky
Reflections of the day
Cross over the noise-filled mind

So many questions
What ifs and regrets
Those moments have since passed
No need to dwell on them or lament

You can't change what was
Or hope it could have been
You can only start from this moment
That you are now in

Allow the power of that silence
To deafen your ears
Let it speak to your soul
And help you surrender to your fears

Accept your humanity
As part of the practice of this life form
Evolve to your highest truth and self
For this is why you were born

Release the need to be
Perfect in your own eyes
For it's through your mistakes
That will help you grow far more wise

Take a moment to have gratitude
For all that comes your way
Even when you feel in heartache
Tell yourself tomorrow is a new day

The Cast of The Sun

When the words do not flow
The heart speaks volumes

When the tears will not release
The pain washes deeply within

When the mind cannot think
The feelings emerge so forcefully

When the belief tells a lie
The soul knows its own truth

When the story is disguised by fear
The writings are crystal clear

When the bars imprison the dream
The door always remains wide open

When the seeker searches endlessly
The lesson awaits to be found

When the day passes so quickly
The moment asks to be cherished

When the grass looks greener on the other side
The cast of the sun changes the perspective in which it is being viewed

*We will never "know it all" for "all we know"
is already within us.*

Trials and Transformation

Anytime you experience transformation, you are going to release the people and things that no longer align with you.

Don't view this as something being "wrong".

Rather that you are right where you are meant to be.

To Rise Through

I know we will get through this
Yet again
But sometimes I wonder
When this tiring cycle will end

Just when I feel
We've come so far
The challenges of my child's health journey
Overwhelms at times my helpless heart

I know our souls are made
To rise through life's storms
But it doesn't mean we won't
Experience deep frustration in this life form

Each turn of my path
I see the wisdom I've imbibed
Knowing more and more
Then I did the last time

It's easy to feel defeated
And question "why me"
But when I'm in my highest self
I accept this is part of mine and my child's soul's journey

And so it is
Another moment in each day
How we choose to resist or accept
Will determine how we lead the way

A Pass in The Road

There comes a pass in the road
When we consciously awake
When the path we've been traversing
Is calling upon a new one for us to take

Something has caught our attention
Enough to make us pause
Re-evaluate how we've been living
Knowing there's a greater cause

This shift will be different
For each and every one
Depending upon the circumstances
Will determine the time in which it comes

For some it's becoming a parent
For others a health scare
For another a job loss
Or someone who just simply dares

When we stop looking outward
To see where the other is
Only then can we attune inward
And decide how we wish to live

See everyone has a purpose
In which they are here to fulfill
The journey is ours for the taking
When we get very clear and still

The more I am evolving
The less I wish to be
Anyone else in the world
Only the truest version of me

Climb Every Mountain

Just when you think
You've conquered the mountain
Another obstacle comes your way
To test your momentum

You may feel it's a "curse"
Or you are being "done to"
But the question I offer is
Will you trust the lesson being offered to you

What perspective will you take
This time around
Where will you stretch in new ways
That you otherwise would have not allowed

Will the story be the same
Inside of your head
Or will you write a new script
That empowers you instead

I know how it feels
To come "so far"
To experience a "setback"
Feeling helpless on where to start

It's easy to feel defeated
Wanting to throw the towel in
Witnessing others forging ahead
As if they are the ones who "win"

The path to self-growth can be arduous
And exhaustive indeed
Yet every new mountain you climb
Is a reflection of your true capacity

There is no race
Or finish line
Your journey is yours alone to take
To be embraced in its own time

So climb every mountain
Greet every obstacle with might
Shift your mindset openly
For the gift of evolution is in the ever-unfolding plight

We cannot heal what we conceal.

Twists and Turns

As we come to the end
Of another unfolding year
Let us reflect upon the moments
That have gotten us here

The "plans" we put into place
Just twelve months ago
Had good intentions behind them
Yet how many do we have to show

We all get caught up
In setting those new year goals
We forge ahead real strong
But then life takes a toll

Unforeseen circumstances
Twists and turns
Leave us feeling empty handed
Exhausted and burned

That doesn't mean
We didn't desire or try
Rather what was meant for us
Had its own place and time

So maybe instead
This time around
We loosen the pressure
And stay open to what is meant to be found

Sure we can still
Set our sights
Move towards our wishes
And even take flight

But if for some reason
We feel a slow start
Take a pause in that moment
And put our hand on our heart

Then ask *The Universe*
"How are you best trying to guide me
Perhaps in a way
I am unable to see"

Listen closely
Watch for the signs
Adjust your "plans"
Let your wings just glide

For where we are meant to land
Maybe different from what we see
Whatever the new year brings us
Is ultimately what is meant to be

This Year

This year had its highs and its lows
It brought moments of deep despair and deep growth
It provided hard lessons for me to learn
It called me to be resilient and be firm

This year has tested my strength
It's broken my spirit so I could find my faith
It has shown me what I'm made of
It has taught me never to give up

This year while coming to an end
Is a reminder that something new is about to begin
Is an example for me to see
Is another chapter in my life's history

This year to come is bound to bring
Far more great and abundant things
A new perspective for me to hold
A new way for my soul to unfold

Time to Awaken

It starts with a whisper
A tug at your heart
Letting you know it is time to awaken
Before you truly fall apart

If you don't hear it
The whisper will become a roar
No longer will it be gentle
Instead it will pound at your door

Screaming *let me in*
I know you're there
You can't hide any longer
Or pretend you don't care

I've waited long enough
For you to see me
It's time you take my hand
And begin your inward journey

You cannot deny its truth
For what you hear is real
So you place your hand on your heart
Willing and ready to show up and feel

What you're suppressing inside
And protecting from others to see
Believing living in your false self
Is better than living authentically

Because no one told you
Or showed you the way
So you follow the masses
Playing it small and safe

No fault of your own
It's what you trusted and knew
Until you realize the madness
You are putting yourself through

It is this pain that gets your attention
And brings you to your knees
Where the whisper within you
Is calling you to see

That the inward journey is a gift
Filled with a treasure of gold
Yours to tap into
And yours to hold

Follow the path of your soul
For it will never lead you astray
It is boundless and beautiful
In every imaginable way

Only when we can get to the root of our pain, can we then heal and nurture the wound itself.

My Mistakes

I am human
I will fail
Yet it is how I move through the fight
Where I will prevail

I must take more breaths and pauses
In my day
When I feel triggered by your doing
In the slightest way

It is not you that I'm resisting
It is my own false beliefs
Expectations at best
That cause my own grief

Of course you feel the projection
Of my intense energy
Taking on more than you should
Because of your incredible empathy

No child should hold the burdens
Of their parents' pain
They should live freely within
Harboring no self-inflicted shame or blame

When I am helpless
I become demanding and unkind
. You call me out on it
As you should it is fine

I am not tired of you
I am tired of me
Repeating these patterns
That cause my own insanity

You may not always feel my love
But I know you know it is there
Because in times of my weakness
You show your unconditional love and care

You are a beautiful soul
Whose heart is beyond measure
Unconditional acceptance
Your essence I treasure

Let us do over
Let us start again
For tomorrow has yet to come
It is this new moment that we can begin

To teach each other how we need to be heard
Understood and held
How offering each other the space to get up
When we take a fall

You have every right to get angry at me
And even push me away
When I am being demanding or unkind
It is how you are trying to convey

Your feelings
Your frustrations
Your emotions
Your fears

I may not always know how to guide you
Through my examples and mistakes
But trust *you* most my dear

If in any way
I made you feel "lesser than"
Please know it is never
My intention

It is my fear that is talking
My scared inner child that projects
For the truth of my heart sees and feels
Your heart as only the best

Change Starts with Us

The world as we know it today
Is a mirror for us to see
Just how disconnected we are
From that of deep inner truth and what's perceived as "reality"

We've created a canvas of lies
Beautifully portrayed and adorned for show
Longing to fit into the constructs of society
All the while hiding behind our own shadow

What we're made to believe is true
By the images flashing across our screen
Couldn't be more false and delusional
Twisting our minds into a robotic machine

Hypnotized by the glamour
Seduced by the fame
So long as we stay numb
We only have ourselves to "blame"

Greed and power have become the ruler
Dictating worthiness and rank
We will continue to be imprisoned by them
If we don't wake up and be the change

And we wonder why our children are suffering
To the degree of pain they feel
They ingest all things from their environment
Not knowing how to discern what's fake and what's real

It's our responsibility to lead by example
To help guide them into their own light
Reminding them not to look externally
Only tap into their divine beauty inside

They need to know they matter
They need to be seen each day
They need to be heard without interruption
They need to trust they are safe and okay

Change first starts with us at home
It's the foundation that holds the walls
It's where our children should always go first
To connect, to share and to be accepted as themselves

Let us empower them to choose wisely
Let us encourage them to attune within
Let us enliven them to rise higher
Let us embody the teachings if we wish for them to truly listen

Through the Journey of Life

We are going to feel loss and gain
Along with joy and pain

These are natural emotions we are to feel
Especially as we move through the journey of life
It becomes that much more real

For the excitement of discovering something new
For the fear of truly seeing it through

For the unknown
For the feeling of deeper love and growth

For what we leave behind
For what we have yet to find

For the memories we once made
For those in which we have yet to create

For the laughter we once shared
For the way we so tenderly cared

For those days when we didn't understand why
For those moments we allowed ourselves a good cry

For thinking we once had it all figured out
For those moments of inevitable doubt

For the enduring love we held through it all
For those times when it was easier to just fall

For in the present moment you are
One with *The Universe*
Now go shine your bright star

It's No Longer Yours to Carry

Along your path of life
You collect the remnants of lack
Passed down through unconsciousness
Of many generations back

What you blindly ingested
What you adopted as your own
You weren't taught to question
Instead you did what you were told

Your parents did their best
With the tools in which they were given
They offered what they could
While providing for their family and making a living

They followed the way they were taught
They suppressed their own fears
And when they projected outwardly to you
They held back their own anxiety and tears

It's no longer yours to carry
It never was to begin
All these years you've been accepting responsibility
Is ultimately where your healing begins

To forgive
To hold compassion
To breathe
To be

It's no longer yours to carry
Now go find a place
Where you can simply let go and release

Climb only your mountain for when you reach your peak,
you will see more clearly the beauty that surrounds you.

How Far We've Come

In this moment
I can truly see
How far we've come
As a family

This path we have walked
Together with great force
Being in fear of those days
Of the unpredictable "emotional big storms"

So many nights
I cried myself to sleep
Praying for answers
To what felt like a mystery

There were so many unknowns
Happening at once
Where to start
I often felt lost

Writing was a place
To express my emotions
Where I often turned
So I didn't feel alone

And through that vessel
Of sharing my pain
I received the clarity
And inner strength

To push through what seemed
Like an endless fight
The Universe sent us an earth angel
To guide our flight

She shared her wisdom
She held the space
She understood it all
Listening to me cry with grace

For the past few years
We have journeyed through
All the healing protocols
And struggles that were not "you"

It wasn't easy
In the least
But we preserved together
And kept the belief

You, my dear child, began to express
How much better you felt
I, too, could see the difference
And could feel my heart melt

Fast forward to now
Some of those days seem a blur
Yet I'm grateful for it all
It has made us all stronger that is for sure

The vibrance you exude
The light that beams from your heart
The way you engage the world
Is what the journey is all about

There is a new calm
A new sense of peace
But it didn't come without
Deep love, trust and endless belief

We love you beautiful one
We honor your soul
A true warrior you are
Infinitely healthy and whole

Thank you for your love
For all that you are
Our spiritual warrior
Our brightest guiding star